£10.00

C000257822

Andrew Atherstone

Day One

Series Editor: Brian H Edwards

The Houses of Parliament
Cradle of democracy

New designs for a new generation

⊚ Strike off the shackles

Parliament prided itself as the champion of liberty, but was slow to promote emancipation for African slaves and Irish Catholics. Both these hard fought campaigns reached a climax in the early 19th century

CONTENTS

© Day One Publications 2011   First printed 2011

A CIP record is held at The British Library   ISBN 978-1-84625-275-4

Published by Day One Publications Ryelands Road, Leominster, HR6 8NZ

☎ 01568 613 740 FAX 01568 611 473 email: sales@dayone.co.uk www.dayone.co.uk   All rights reserved

sign: Kathryn Chedgzoy   Printed by Polskabook, UK

dication: for Paul, Joy, Thomas and Beth Mawdesley

Welcome to the Houses of Parliament

The Houses of Parliament are among the most iconic buildings in the world; they are a World Heritage Site. Their grand neo-gothic vista dominating the River Thames at Westminster is the focus of the United Kingdom's parliamentary democracy, resonant with historic associations. John Bright (Quaker politician and reformer) famously declared in the 1860s that 'England is the Mother of Parliaments'. The Westminster model of democracy has been widely exported and imitated around the globe, especially in parts of the former British Empire.

The Houses of Parliament have always been at the centre of national events. Here Sir Thomas More and King Charles I stood on trial prior to their executions, and here also Guy Fawkes and his co-conspirators launched their audacious Gunpowder Plot to destroy the king and

his advisors at one stroke. It was here that the nation's great orators have clashed in the House of Commons, a witness to the intense parliamentary rivalries of William Pitt against Charles James Fox, and Benjamin Disraeli against William Gladstone, among many others. The buildings have been brought to ruins by devastating fire in the 1830s and the bombs of the Luftwaffe in the 1940s, only to rise from the ashes. And here crowds of protesters have gathered at the gates to demand the admission of their representatives to the parliamentary fold: Roman Catholics, Chartists, secularists and suffragettes. Monarchs lie in state here, and in these buildings one Prime Minister was shot through the heart.

Here, Britain's national identity is forged and its democracy continues to mature. This is the story of the Houses of Parliament.

Above: *The Houses of Parliament, from the South Bank, Lambeth*

1 King and council

For more than a millennium, Parliament, monarchy and the Christian church have been inextricably bound together at Westminster geographically and politically. First came the abbey, then the royal palace, and finally the offices of government

Westminster, as the name suggests, first rose to prominence as the site of an influential Christian community. The place was originally called Thorney Island, the island of thorns or brambles on the muddy floodplain of the River Thames. Perhaps its very inaccessibility and bleakness attracted the first Christian monks. A Benedictine abbey was founded here in the 960s by Archbishop Dunstan of Canterbury, with the support of King Edgar. Thorney abbey soon became known as the West Minster, to distinguish it from the East Minster (St Paul's Cathedral) rebuilt during the same period further down the Thames in the City of London.

Westminster Abbey attracted major royal patronage throughout the 11th century. King Cnut donated precious Christian relics as proof of his religious devotion and, according to some medieval manuscripts, his famous attempt to turn back the tide took place on the shore of the Thames at Westminster. Cnut's son and heir, Harold Harefoot who died in March 1040, asked to be buried here rather than at Winchester; he was the first monarch to be interred in the abbey though his corpse was exhumed by his half-brother, King Harthacnut, and thrown into the Thames.

Edward the Confessor, the last Saxon king of England, firmly established Westminster's pre-eminence. As a sign of his Christian piety, he devoted considerable energy to rebuilding

Above: William the Conqueror, from the Royal Gallery

Facing page: The glittering throne dominates the House of Lords, a reminder that Parliament depends on royal authority

the abbey, which was consecrated amidst great celebration on the Feast of the Holy Innocents, 28 December 1065. A few days later Edward died and was buried before the high altar where his tomb became a shrine. A year later, William of Normandy conquered England at the Battle of Hastings and explicitly identified himself with Edward's legacy in order to legitimize his claim to the throne. William was crowned on Christmas Day 1066 in Westminster Abbey, the venue for every English coronation since. He chose Edward's palace at Westminster as his principal home, a decision which was to determine the future location of the British Parliament.

The Conqueror's heir, William Rufus, enhanced Westminster Palace by adding a Great Hall in the 1090s, a feat of Norman engineering. It was a giant status symbol, demonstrating the king's royal magnificence and intended to astonish his subjects and rivals. Measuring 240 feet (73 metres) by 68 feet (20 metres) it was by far the largest hall in England, and probably in Europe. When one of his servants observed flatteringly that it was much larger than they would ever need, William replied that it was 'not half large enough'. The king boasted that the hall was 'a mere bedchamber compared with what I had intended to build.' It was used for royal feasts and pageantry and established Westminster as the chief royal residence, towering above its neighbours. Despite the rigours of fire and war, the medieval hall still survives today at the centre of the Houses of Parliament. No other building in the world has been continuously connected for so many centuries with a nation's political life.

Below: Westminster Hall, built by William Rufus in the 11th century as a royal status symbol

Above: King John assents to Magna Carta *under pressure from the barons at Runnymede, from a mural in St Stephen's Hall*

From Witenagemot to Parliament

In Anglo-Saxon times, the English kings gathered together the most respected leaders of the community in the *Witenagemot* or *Witan* ('assembly of the wise') to discuss questions of national significance. The Norman and Plantagenet monarchs followed suit, summoning councils to offer advice. These meetings were called and dismissed at the whim of the king, who decided the agenda, location and membership.

During the 1230s the word 'Parliament' (*parliamentum* in Latin, or *parlement* in French) was used for the first time to describe major meetings of the royal council. It soon replaced earlier names like *consilium* or *colloquium*. 'Parliament' originally signified an informal dialogue, or 'parley', but it came to refer to the official business of the state. Parliament gathered wherever the king chose. It was often summoned to different parts of the country, depending on the location of the royal court. Under the Plantagenets it met in cities such as Oxford, Lincoln, York, Gloucester, Northampton, Cambridge, Winchester, Leicester and Shrewsbury. Only later did Westminster become Parliament's regular home.

Plantagenet Parliaments were fluid in their composition. The key secular and ecclesiastical leaders were usually invited, including dukes, earls, barons, bishops and abbots. Knights from the shires (counties) and burgesses from the major towns (boroughs) first attended in the 1260s at the instigation of Baron Simon de Montfort, and were always summoned after 1325. Popular representation of local communities gradually became more significant, especially when

Above: Baron Marochetti's bronze statue of Richard Coeur de Lion in the Old Palace Yard. It was originally displayed at the 1851 Great Exhibition

the king needed to raise taxation. These groups slowly developed into the Lords and the Commons, the Upper and the Lower House. The early Plantagenet kings felt under no obligation to seek their subjects' consent before making new laws, but they soon discovered that the promulgation of statutes in Parliament made the legislation more effective.

The Great Charter of Liberties

In times of turmoil, the king's council was not afraid to challenge royal authority. Most notably, the violent clash between King John and the aristocracy in the early 13th century led to the creation of one of the defining documents of British parliamentary government, *Magna Carta*, the 'Great Charter of Liberties'. John had alienated the English barons by his despotic rule and his thirst for wealth. He was a failure on the battlefield, unlike his older brother Richard Coeur de Lion, and was also accused of extorting huge sums from his subjects by taxes and fines. Growing resentment amongst the barons led to rebellion, until the king agreed to negotiate. In June 1215 he signed *Magna Carta* at Runnymede Meadow, by the River Thames, between Windsor Castle and the rebel camp at Staines. It made a number of concessions over baronial grievances and established some key constitutional principles.

The Archbishop of Canterbury, Stephen Langton, acted as mediator between the king and the barons, and his influence is seen in the opening section which declares, '*Anglicana ecclesia libera sit*' ('The English church shall be free'). Other sections addressed financial and judicial corruption, as well as specific concerns such as royal forests, fishing, weights and measures, and foreign mercenaries. Later interpreters found in *Magna Carta* the roots of basic rights like trial by jury and freedom from arbitrary arrest (*habeas corpus*). It showed that the king was answerable to the rule of law just like everyone lse, and that his law-making and tax-raising powers required the consent of his subjects. No sooner had John signed and sealed the document than he repudiated it. Pope Innocent III believed it was an infringement of the monarch's God-given authority, so he annulled the charter. He denounced it as 'not only shameful and demeaning but also illegal and unjust', claiming that the rebels had forced John to accept it by 'violence and fear'.

The basic principles of *Magna Carta*, especially its defence of the inviolable liberties of the king's subjects, became deeply embedded in English consciousness. It was seen as a fundamental foundation of all parliamentary legislation. The charter was renewed by John's son, Henry III, in a definitive version of 1225 and was confirmed over forty times during the next two centuries. Political reformers in every generation have turned to the charter for vindication of their ideals,

especially when challenging the authority of the monarch or the ruling elite. The historian William Stubbs, writing at the time of great parliamentary reforms in the 1870s, went so far as to claim that 'The whole of the constitutional history of England is little more than a commentary on *Magna Carta*'. In the House of Lords today, statues of the sixteen barons and two bishops present at Runnymede look down upon the proceedings, as a permanent reminder to the peers of the ancient liberties of British citizens.

Seeking justice

Alongside legislation and taxation, the most significant function of the early English Parliaments was the dispensing of justice. It was the highest court in the land, where petitioners went to present their cases before the king. However, because Parliament was often not in session, and because the royal household wandered like nomads, it was sometimes impossible to

Left: King Henry III renews and confirms Magna Carta in Westminster Hall in 1225

Left: Benjamin West's painting from 1784 of Moses receiving the tablets from God on Mount Sinai. It now hangs in Westminster Hall, near the original law courts, symbolizing the close relationship between the Ten Commandments and the British legal system

win a fair hearing. In response to this grievance, *Magna Carta* decreed that litigation must be heard not by a travelling tribunal but in a fixed place, so Westminster Hall was set aside for lawyers and judges.

The Court of the King's Bench, the Court of Common Pleas and later the Court of Chancery took up residence in the Hall, separated by temporary timber partitions which could be dismantled when the venue was needed for grand state banquets. Near the Hall was the Court of the Star Chamber, so called because it had stars on the ceiling, which dealt with serious cases such as rioting and sedition. Under the Tudors and Stuarts the Star Chamber became a byword for tyranny and the persecution of political opponents, so it was abolished by the Long Parliament under Charles I in 1641. The other courts continued in these cramped and noisy conditions

until new rooms were built next to Westminster Hall in 1826 by Sir John Soane. They finally moved away from the parliamentary estate in 1882 when the Royal Courts of Justice were opened on the Strand.

Parliament remained the highest court in the land, the ultimate source of justice in Britain, until the end of the 20th century. It took precedence over all lower courts and its judicial functions were vested in the Lords of Appeal (known as the 'Law Lords'), a panel of twelve professional judges with seats in the House of Lords. These judicial powers were abolished by the Constitutional Reform Act of 2005 which established the Supreme Court of the United Kingdom. After many centuries, the historic connection between Parliament and the judiciary was now at an end.

The Speaker

With his familiar cry of 'Order! Order!', the Speaker presides over debates in the House of Commons today. This influential position originated in the reign of Edward III in the 1370s, when the king summoned Parliament to Westminster to raise funds for his military exploits in France. The Commons were sent away to consult by themselves in the Chapter House at the abbey, where the knights and burgesses denounced the corruption of the king's ministers and the evils of heavy taxation. One of the knights from Herefordshire, Sir Peter de la Mare, took the initiative in steering the Commons towards a consensus and in summarizing their opinions. Therefore he was commissioned to speak on their behalf before the Lords, and is recognised as the first 'Speaker'. The Speaker's symbol of authority is the mace, a popular weapon of war during the Middle Ages.

As the Commons grew in influence, so the position of the Speaker rose in prestige. An Act of Parliament in the late 17th century declared that he was the 'First Commoner of the Realm', next in rank to the peers. He rode in a state coach and by the 1790s enjoyed an official residence within the Palace of Westminster.

Today the Speaker is expected to be completely impartial, in effect to have 'retired' from party politics. By tradition his constituency seat is uncontested by the major parties at general elections. The last Speaker ousted by a vote in the House of Commons was Charles Manners-Sutton (son of an Archbishop of Canterbury) in 1835, who was accused by the Whigs of being biased towards the Tories.

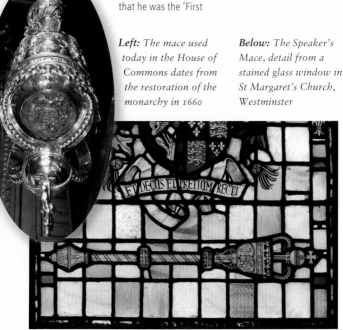

Left: *The mace used today in the House of Commons dates from the restoration of the monarchy in 1660*

Below: *The Speaker's Mace, detail from a stained glass window in St Margaret's Church, Westminster*

Status symbols

During the 13th and 14th centuries Westminster continued to grow in dominance as the primary centre of national political life. This was partly a deliberate strategy by the Plantagenet kings. For example, Henry III wanted to forge an alliance, both ideological and geographical, between monarch, church and government. He invested in both Westminster Palace and Westminster Abbey in order to demonstrate the dynastic roots and spiritual prerogative of his royal power. Henry added new apartments to the palace from the 1220s, including the Painted Chamber, a reception room with murals of Old Testament narratives.

From 1245 Henry rebuilt the abbey at astronomical cost, transferring Edward the Confessor's bones to a new shrine decorated with the crown jewels. He was especially devoted to the cult of the Confessor as the model of kingly piety, and he chose Edward as England's patron saint (later trumped by St George). Henry was buried in the abbey next to his hero, establishing a tradition which further strengthened the links between Westminster and the monarchy.

Henry's son, Edward I, enhanced the status of Westminster by building a magnificent new chapel for his palace. There was already a private chapel, dedicated to the first Christian martyr, St Stephen (Acts 7), but the king was unimpressed by its modest size so he demolished it in 1292. He believed that Westminster deserved a much grander structure to compete with *La Sainte-Chapelle* ('The Holy Chapel') erected in the 1240s by King Louis IX in the centre of Paris. Edward's chapel (St Stephen's Chapel) deliberately mirrored its Parisian rival, with its two-storey structure, vast windows and sumptuous gothic detail. It was not complete until the reign of his grandson, Edward III, who financed its lavish decoration

Above: *St Stephen's Chapel, built in the early 14th century as England's answer to La Sainte-Chapelle in Paris*

in the 1340s with the spoils of war from victories against the French. The king also founded a religious college at Westminster, consisting of a dean, twelve secular canons, twelve vicars, four clerks and six choristers. Their responsibility was to pray for the souls of the royal family and they were given St Stephen's Chapel as their collegiate church. The chapel was to play a major role in the history of Parliament when it

Top: The lower storey of St Stephen's Chapel was a Lady Chapel, known today as St Mary's Undercroft. It was restored as Parliament's chapel in the 1840s

Above: The baptistery in St Mary's Undercroft

Left: Carved roof boss in St Mary's Undercroft showing the boiling of St John the Evangelist in a cauldron of oil, an apocryphal story

Left: An angelic roof boss in St Mary's Undercroft

Above: *The hamerbeam roof of Westminster Hall is carried by a company of angels*

became the seat of the House of Commons during the Edwardian Reformation in the 16th century.

Westminster's political status reached a new peak in the 1390s during the reign of Richard II, who remodelled Westminster Hall to illustrate his belief in the divine vocation of the monarchy. He commissioned thirteen statues of all the English kings since Edward the Confessor, decorated with gilded crowns and emerald green robes. Six of them were set up in niches in the south wall, like a reredos (the ornamental screen behind the altar) in a medieval cathedral, looking down upon Richard's royal throne. At great expense the king also replaced the old Norman roof with an innovative hammerbeam structure, made from oak and weighing 660 tons. At the end of each beam

Lying in State

The long relationship between Westminster Hall and the British monarchy has been expressed in a new tradition since the beginning of the 20th century with the 'lying in state' of deceased monarchs and their consorts, to allow the public to pay their last respects. Five kings and queens have been honoured in this way: Edward VII (1910), George V (1936), George VI (1952), Queen Mary (1953) and Queen Elizabeth the Queen Mother (2002). An estimated 200,000 people filed passed the Queen Mother's coffin, forming a queue several miles long.

Two of Britain's greatest Prime Ministers have also lain in state at Westminster Hall, William Gladstone in 1898 (before his state funeral in Westminster Abbey) and Winston Churchill in 1965. The coffins of the forty-eight passengers and crew who lost their lives in the R101 airship disaster were also laid here after their repatriation. The R101 was an innovative hydrogen airship, under the command of Captain Irwin and First Officer Atherstone, which crashed at Beauvais in France on its maiden voyage to India in October 1930.

Below: Crowds file passed the coffin of Queen Elizabeth the Queen Mother, lying in state at Westminster Hall in April 2002

was a carved angel watching over the royal court below, as if providing a heavenly mandate for Richard's government.

Ironically, it was in this very hall that Richard II was deposed in 1399 by his cousin, Henry Bolingbroke (Henry IV), as English politics degenerated into anarchy, vendetta, betrayal and the Wars of the Roses.

Left: One of the statues of early English kings in Westminster Hall, erected by Richard II in the 1390s. Their orbs, sceptres and swords are Victorian replacements

Right and inset: The white hart, symbol of Richard II, appears throughout Westminster Hall

Royal palaces

Since the days of Edward the Confessor in the 11th century, Westminster Palace had been predominantly a royal residence and only occasionally the venue for Parliament, which met seldom and briefly. Yet there was a significant shift in focus during the reign of Henry VIII, England's renaissance king. In 1512 a fire rampaged through the palace, destroying much of the monarch's private quarters. Instead of repairing the damage, Henry simply moved out. In 1529 he confiscated nearby York Place (known as Whitehall Palace) after the downfall of his chief political adviser, Cardinal Wolsey, Archbishop of York. This magnificent residence, one of the grandest in the capital, was built as a rival to Lambeth Palace on the other side of the river, the London home of the Archbishop of Canterbury. With this ready-made palace fit for a king, Henry no longer needed his ruined lodgings at Westminster, which were demolished. All the surviving buildings were therefore given over to the functions of government as an administrative and legal centre, and as the permanent home of the English Parliament.

Whitehall was considerably enlarged under the Stuart kings, becoming the grandest royal palace in Europe, but it too burned down in 1698 during the reign of William and Mary. St James' Palace, erected by Henry VIII, was therefore the principal residence for the Hanoverian

Nevertheless, there is still a State Bed in the State Bedroom, in the official residence of the Speaker of the House of Commons, just in case the monarch should choose to stay the night.

The Houses of Parliament still retain their status as a royal palace today, and therefore the Royal Standard replaces the Union Jack on top of the Victoria Tower whenever the Queen is present. The site was controlled for centuries by the monarch's representative, the Lord Great Chamberlain, until responsibility for the bulk of the estate was handed over to the Commons and the Lords in 1965. The suite of chambers comprising the Queen's processional route at the State Opening of Parliament remains under royal jurisdiction.

kings. Buckingham Palace, built by the Duke of Buckingham, was bought by George III in 1761 as a wedding present for his new wife, Queen Charlotte. Not until 1837 did the young Queen Victoria transfer the monarch's official London home from St James' Palace to Buckingham Palace.

Even after Henry VIII's departure it remained tradition until the Civil War for a new monarch to sleep at Westminster Palace before coronation in the abbey the following day. George IV briefly revived this practice in 1820, but was the last to do so.

DIEV ET MON DROIT

With This Ring I was Wedded to The Realm.

② Gunpowder, treason and plot

Although Henry VIII loosened the monarch's personal ties with Westminster by abandoning the palace, he greatly enhanced the status of Parliament during the political and religious upheaval of the Reformation

Henry VIII was determined to ensure the dynastic survival of the Tudors by providing a male heir to the throne. His marriage to Katherine of Aragon produced only one surviving child, despite several pregnancies, and precipitated a national crisis. Cardinal Wolsey was set the task of negotiating an annulment of the royal marriage with the Pope, but he failed to find a breakthrough via the normal diplomatic channels and was dismissed from office in 1529. Instead, the king turned to Parliament as the tool he needed to bring about constitutional and religious change. It was an innovative strategy and a turning point in parliamentary history. It set a precedent by elevating statute law above every other authority, even the authority of the church itself.

The break with Rome

In March 1532 the Commons presented the king with a petition, known as the *Supplication Against the Ordinaries*, which laid down numerous grievances against the church. The clergy resisted this parliamentary interference which led Henry ominously to observe that they had divided loyalties between Rome and England and were 'but half our subjects, yea, and scarce our subjects'. Faced by these thinly-veiled threats, the church leadership surrendered to royal authority which provoked Thomas More, the Lord Chancellor and a papal loyalist, to resign in despair.

Above: The divorce proceedings of Henry VIII and Katherine of Aragon before a papal tribunal, one of a number of Tudor scenes painted in 1910 for the Houses of Parliament

Facing page: The Commons petitioning Queen Elizabeth to marry, painted in 1911 by Solomon J. Solomon for the Committee Staircase

Over the next two years a raft of new legislation gave the force of law to this shift in authority from pope to king. Parliament put an end to the financial payment of 'annates' or 'first-fruits' from English bishops to the pope, forbade appeals to the ecclesiastical courts in Rome, and gave the crown the right to appoint bishops (a right the British monarch still enjoys today). The pinnacle of this legislation was the Act of Supremacy, passed in November 1534, which declared the king to be 'the only Supreme Head in earth of the Church of England'. This Act gave him the right to reform the doctrine and ceremonies of the church, in order to expunge 'all errors, heresies, and other enormities and abuses' and to promote 'virtue in Christ's religion'. It made the break with Rome complete. Meanwhile the Act of Succession forced the king's subjects to acknowledge his new wife, Anne Boleyn, as queen and her children as the rightful heirs to the throne.

Sometimes Henry and his chief adviser, Thomas Cromwell, used strong-arm tactics to force through religious change. For example, when the Commons proved reluctant to suppress the monasteries, the king threatened them with violence. Henry summoned an influential MP and grabbed him by the ear saying, 'Get my Bill passed by tomorrow, or else tomorrow this head of yours will be off!' Cromwell insisted that 'the great and fat abbots' must be removed from their monasteries; as a result they were also removed from the House of Lords.

The dissolution thus led to a fundamental shift in the balance between Lords Spiritual and Lords Temporal in the Upper House. During the previous reign 48 spiritual peers were regularly summoned to Parliament, but never more than 43 lay peers. Yet when the abbots and priors were thrown out, the number of Lords Spiritual fell by more than half, leaving only the bishops and archbishops to speak on behalf of the church. Henceforth these clergymen

Above: Confrontation between Cardinal Wolsey and Sir Thomas More over a royal subsidy in 1523, part of the 'Building of Britain' series in St Stephen's Hall

would always be a dwindling minority in the House of Lords. A century later there were 126 lay peers in the Lords, and today there are approximately 700, but still only 26 spiritual peers.

Those who refused to abandon their allegiance to the pope were hurried to execution. The most prominent prisoners were Sir Thomas More and Cardinal John Fisher, who were both put on trial in Westminster Hall in the summer of 1535 for refusing to swear the oaths required by the Act of Succession and the Act of Supremacy. More was the only layman in the country to resist, for fear of condemning 'my soul to perpetual damnation'. At his trial he rejected the royal supremacy as 'directly repugnant to the laws of God and his holy church', and warned that Parliament was flying in the face of Catholic Christendom. He announced: 'I have, for every bishop of yours, above one hundred; and for one council or Parliament of yours … I have all the councils made these thousand years. And for this one kingdom, I have all other Christian realms.' Nevertheless, before being carried to the scaffold at the Tower of London, his parting words were conciliatory: 'Though your Lordships have

now here in earth been judges to my condemnation, we may yet hereafter in heaven merrily all meet together, to our everlasting satisfaction.'

The plagues of Job

Henry VIII's children, Edward VI, Mary I and Elizabeth I, followed the precedent set by their father in enforcing religious change by parliamentary statute. This had the effect of fixing Parliament firmly at the centre of national life during the intense Reformation controversies. It was in session almost every year between 1529 and 1559. One of Elizabeth's royal advisers, who preferred to operate without the consent of MPs, likened frequent Parliaments to 'the plagues of Job', but they were here to stay.

During Edward's reign, the 1549 and 1552 Acts of Uniformity introduced a reformed and vernacular liturgy throughout the Church of England (replacing Latin with English); this was

Right: Bishop Hugh Latimer preaches before King Edward VI at St Paul's Cross, painted in 1910. The portrait of Latimer was said to be modelled on William Booth, founder of the Salvation Army

Above: *Edward VI, the boy-king who ushered in the English Reformation, one of many royal statues in the Palace of Westminster*

that MPs bore significant responsibility for the spiritual life of the nation. Indeed one MP, John Hooker, wrote in 1572 that the main justification for Parliament's existence was to see 'that God be honoured'.

Under the Tudor dynasty, both the Lords and the Commons were given a dedicated room in the Palace of Westminster for the first time, a sign of Parliament's increasing importance. The Lords met in the White Chamber, which they continued to occupy until the 19th century. The Commons were granted permanent use of St Stephen's Chapel after the college of canons was dissolved by the Second Chantries Act of 1547. Both Houses took on a corporate identity and began to keep journals of their proceedings.

This takeover of the chapel was of unexpected significance in shaping Britain's parliamentary democracy because of its architectural layout. Rows of benches faced each other across the aisle, designed for collegiate prayer and choral worship, which forced the Commons to debate face-to-face in an adversarial manner and thus contributed to the development of a two-party political system. Today it remains impossible for MPs to shift their allegiance between the government and the opposition without crossing the floor of the House for all to see. The Speaker's chair was set up on the altar steps, which perhaps explains why MPs traditionally bow to the chair as they enter the chamber, as they bowed in reverence to the altar in the 16th century. The House of

the first time that Christian worship had been prescribed by Parliament. Under Mary, the nation was reunited with Rome in November 1554 when the Commons and the Lords knelt in tears before the papal legate, Cardinal Pole, and asked forgiveness for their misdemeanours. Two months later they revived the old medieval heresy laws, *De Haeretico Comburendo* ('On the Burning of Heretics'), which allowed the execution of almost three hundred evangelicals, both men and women.

The pendulum swung back in the opposite direction under Elizabeth, who used Parliament to usher in the so-called Elizabethan Settlement of 1559 which established the Church of England as Protestant and reformed by law. During these topsy-turvy years of theological debate, it became an accepted tradition

Right: Queen Elizabeth I seated on the throne in the House of Lords in the 1580s, with the Commons in attendance

Below: A Victorian statue of Elizabeth I, from the Royal Gallery

ELIZABETH

Commons today, built by Charles Barry in the 1840s and rebuilt by Giles Gilbert Scott in the 1940s, still deliberately mirrors the size and shape of a Christian chapel.

Terrorist conspiracies

The death of Queen Elizabeth in March 1603 brought the Tudor dynasty to an end and the start of a new regime. The crown was offered to James VI of Scotland, aged 36, who was now acclaimed as James I of England. He sought to promote Anglo-Scottish integration, perhaps even the union of the Westminster and Edinburgh Parliaments, though this was not achieved for another century.

There were wide expectations that James would inaugurate a new era of religious toleration after the deep divisions of the Reformation period. His Catholic subjects in particular hoped for repeal of the repressive Elizabethan statutes against recusancy (those who refused as a matter of conscience to attend Protestant worship, from the Latin *recusare*, to refuse). The king told his secretary of state: 'I will never allow in my conscience that the blood of any man shall be shed for diversity of opinions in religion.' His mother, Mary Queen of Scots, had been a lifelong Catholic and his young wife, Anne of

Left and below: The lion and the unicorn in the House of Lords, heraldic symbols from the royal coat of arms representing England and Scotland respectively

Denmark, had recently converted to Catholicism from Lutheranism. These were hopeful signs for the beleaguered recusant community. Yet, by the time James called his first Parliament in March 1604 the mood had changed, partly as a result of the 'Bye Plot' and 'Main Plot' to topple the king. He now told the gathered MPs that the peace of the nation depended upon 'profession of the true religion' and urged the bishops in the House of Lords to be more 'careful, vigilant, and diligent than you have been to win souls to God.' The penal anti-Catholic legislation was not repealed but confirmed.

Catholic dismay at the tone of this first Stuart Parliament led directly to the Gunpowder Plot. On Sunday 20 May 1604 five men met in secret at the Duck and Drake Inn, on the Strand, where they hatched a plan to blow up the House of Lords, together with the king and his government. The driving force amongst this band of conspirators was Robert Catesby, from a wealthy recusant family in Warwickshire, and he soon drew a dozen men into its web. Their basic objective was terrifyingly simple: to cause a huge explosion at the next scheduled Opening of Parliament in February 1605. The king would certainly be present, along with England's chief politicians and bishops, and perhaps other members of the royal family like Prince Henry, the young heir to the throne. This assassination of the national leadership would be followed by an uprising in the midlands. Nine year-old Princess Elizabeth, James' daughter, would be kidnapped and proclaimed as queen, while a Catholic Protector would rule the country during her minority. Catesby declared that the destruction of Parliament was a fitting punishment, because 'in that place have they done us all the mischief.'

In the early 17th century the area around the Houses of Parliament was a complex jumble of properties, which had grown up randomly without modern concerns about security. Private homes, storerooms, lodging houses, taverns and shops jostled for space amongst the law courts and Parliament buildings. It was therefore easy for the conspirators to get close to their target. One of the plotters, Thomas Percy, arranged to hire a house in Westminster from John Whynniard (keeper of the king's wardrobe). It had a large cellar or storeroom, probably part of the old medieval kitchen of the ancient palace, situated directly under the House of Lords. Over the next few months barrels of gunpowder were secretly shipped across the Thames from Catesby's lodgings in Lambeth and hidden in the cellar.

The plot betrayed

If the Opening of Parliament had gone ahead as expected in February 1605, the terrorist outrage might have succeeded with the death of the monarch and his councillors. As it happened, Parliament was postponed until November, partly because of fears of the plague in London. This gave the conspirators an unexpected extra nine months in which to perfect their plans,

but it also meant there was greater likelihood of mistakes or betrayal. In late August they discovered that the gunpowder had 'decayed', so they had to find a replacement supply. With twice as many barrels now crowded into the cellar, concealment was more difficult.

Everything went to plan until 26 October 1605, just ten days before Parliament was due to meet. That evening Lord Monteagle received an anonymous note at his home in Hoxton in north London, handed to his servant by a stranger in the street. It urged the peer to flee from the capital for safety and to avoid the Opening of Parliament at all costs: 'My Lord, out of the love I bear to some of your friends, I have a care of your preservation. Therefore I would advise you, as you tender your life, to devise some excuse to shift your attendance at this

Below: Westminster in the 17th century was dominated by the Parliament House, the Hall and the Abbey. Westminster Bridge, across the River Thames, was not built until the 1740s

Above: *An 18th century sketch of the storeroom below the old Palace of Westminster, used by the Gunpowder conspirators but destroyed by fire in 1834*

Parliament; for God and man hath concurred to punish the wickedness of this time. ... For though there be no appearance of any stir, yet I say they shall receive a terrible blow this Parliament; and yet they shall not see who hurts them.'

Was it a hoax or a sinister warning? The letter is still preserved amongst the State Papers in the National Archives, but its authorship remains a mystery. Some have even suggested that Monteagle wrote it himself, to deflect attention away from his connections with the conspirators. Its discovery turned him at once into a national hero. Although it was late at night, Monteagle rode straight to Whitehall to bring the letter to the attention of Robert Cecil (Earl of Salisbury). Salisbury took the threat seriously, but refrained from making arrests. As England's grand spymaster, it is possible he already knew about the plot and was waiting to catch as many terrorists as possible. Meanwhile Catesby, warned by Monteagle's servant that his plans had been betrayed, chose to push ahead regardless.

A 'thundering sin of fire and brimstone'

On Monday 4 November, the day before the Opening of Parliament, the authorities made a thorough search of the buildings around Westminster. Suspicions were aroused when they discovered large piles of firewood in a local cellar, far more than was needed for heating or cooking in the small house above. Furthermore the tenant, Thomas Percy, was known to have his main residence elsewhere. Behind the firewood were thirty-six barrels containing eighteen hundredweight of gunpowder (almost a ton), enough to blow the House of Lords sky high. Around midnight a man was arrested skulking in the shadows, and gave his name only as John Johnson, Percy's servant. Under interrogation he admitted that he wanted to destroy the king and the lords, but that the devil was responsible for foiling the plan.

In panic, the other conspirators fled from London under cover of darkness, with the authorities in hot pursuit. Their dream of a Catholic uprising in the midlands in the wake of the Westminster explosion proved illusory. After a day's manic riding they reached the sanctuary of Holbeache House, at Kingswinford in Staffordshire, where they were besieged the next day by a militia led by Sir Richard Walsh, high sheriff of Worcestershire. The plotters were vastly outnumbered and soon overpowered. Four were shot and killed, including Catesby and Percy. Others were captured, though some managed to escape and went on the run. The corpses of Catesby and Percy were decapitated and their heads displayed on London Bridge.

Meanwhile at the Tower of London, 'John Johnson' was broken by torture at the command of the king (although expressly forbidden by *Magna Carta*). He was hung up by manacles and possibly also stretched on the rack. Faced by this agony, the captive soon began to confess. He divulged numerous details of the plot and revealed that his true name was Guy Fawkes, a Catholic from Yorkshire who had spent the previous decade as a mercenary fighting for the Spanish in the Netherlands.

After recovering from the initial shock of the terrorist plot, King James went ahead with the Opening of Parliament a few days late, on 9 November. He was quick to remind the assembled peers not to make the mistake of connecting Catholicism and conspiracy, since only a small minority were guilty of the recent outrage. He observed that if the gunpowder had exploded he would at least have had the consolation of perishing 'in the most honourable and best company' rather than in a brothel or alehouse. Nevertheless the king called the attempted murder

Below: Facsimile of the mysterious letter sent to Lord Monteagle, now in the National Archives

of so many innocent people 'a roaring, nay a thundering sin of fire and brimstone' from which God had miraculously delivered them. He exhorted Parliament to thankfulness for this divine preservation from their enemies, exclaiming like King David in the Old Testament: 'The mercy of God is above all his works' (Psalm 145:9).

James told the Venetian ambassador that because the plotters had attempted to dethrone him, he was now 'obliged to stain my hands with their blood, sorely against my will.' The surviving conspirators were quickly captured, and a number of their relatives and confidants were brought down with them. The government would not rest until they had rooted out anyone connected with the affair. Some died in custody, others were executed, mostly after torture. The Tower of London was the centre of the interrogations, where Sir William Waad (the lieutenant governor) saw his work in spiritual terms. He erected a monument to the plot's discovery with words in Hebrew from the Old Testament: 'God reveals the deep things of darkness and brings the shadow of death into the light' (Job 12:22).

Hung, drawn and quartered

The trial of the eight men at the heart of the plot took place on 27 January 1606 in Westminster Hall, next to the House of Lords they had sought to destroy. It was a show trial witnessed by the king and queen, parliamentary dignitaries, foreign ambassadors and a crowd of eager spectators. The verdict was never in doubt. Sir Edward Phelips (Speaker of the House of Commons) announced that they were guilty of an act of treason 'of such

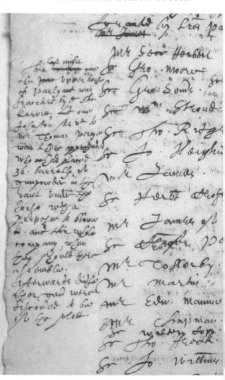

Above: Entry in the margin of the Commons Journal for 5 November 1605, recording the discovery of the Gunpowder Plot. A copy hangs in the 'Noes' lobby of the House of Commons

Above: The chief conspirators in the Gunpowder Plot, from a contemporary print. Catesby, Fawkes and Percy are second, third and fourth from the right

horror and monstrous nature, that before now, the tongue of man never delivered, the ear of man never heard, the heart of man never conceived, nor the malice of hellish or earthly devil never practised.' He abhorred the attempt 'to murder and subvert such a king, such a queen, such a prince, such a progeny, such a state, such a government, so complete and absolute, that God approves, the world admires, all true English hearts honour and reverence.' Next, Sir Edward Coke (the Attorney-General) explained at length that the prisoners deserved to be hung, drawn and quartered, with their hearts torn out and their dismembered bodies exposed as 'prey for the fowls of the air'.

The only prisoner to plead guilty was Sir Everard Digby, a young gentleman in his late twenties who had been drawn into the plot by Catesby. Although Digby had been knighted in April 1603 during the king's progress south from Scotland, he had grown disillusioned with royal policy. He told the court that compared to his religion everything else took second place,

whether 'his estate, his life, his name, his memory, his posterity, and worldly and earthly felicity'. Yet when he appealed to his judges to have compassion upon his wife and infant sons, Coke hit back with a stark judgement from the book of Psalms: 'Let his wife be a widow, and his children vagabonds, let his posterity be destroyed, and in the next generation let his name be quite put out' (Psalm 109:9–13).

The trial lasted only one day and all eight prisoners were found guilty of high treason. Early the next morning four of them, including Digby, were dragged on hurdles to the churchyard at St Paul's Cathedral where they were hung, drawn and quartered. The remaining convicts suffered the same fate the following day in the Old Palace Yard at Westminster. The government deliberately chose to execute them in the very place they had sought to destroy. Guy Fawkes was the last to climb the scaffold from where he asked forgiveness of the king and Parliament. When he was hung, his neck broke, so he was spared the conscious torment of the disembowelment which followed.

Public thanksgiving

In January 1606, a week before the execution of the chief plotters, a Thanksgiving Bill was initiated in the House of Commons by Sir Edward Montagu, a leading puritan MP from Northamptonshire. It decreed that public thanksgiving be made to God every 5 November for the king's deliverance from the Gunpowder Plot. This annual celebration was soon marked across the country with bonfires, fireworks, the ringing of church bells and the burning of effigies of Guy Fawkes.

The Church of England developed a special liturgy for the occasion, praising God's 'wonderful and mighty deliverance'. These annual prayers recalled that the royal family and members of Parliament were 'by popish treachery appointed as sheep to the slaughter, in a most barbarous and savage manner, beyond the examples of former ages.' Congregations across the country declared, 'From this unnatural conspiracy not our merit but thy mercy, not our foresight but thy providence delivered us. And therefore not unto us, O Lord, not unto us, but unto thy name be ascribed all honour and glory.' Many clergy preached annual Bonfire Sermons, often expounding the Apostle Paul's exhortation to obey the governing authorities (Romans 13) or Jesus Christ's declaration that 'the Son of Man is not come to destroy men's lives, but to save them' (Luke 9:56).

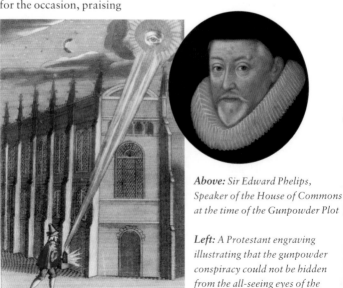

Above: Sir Edward Phelips, Speaker of the House of Commons at the time of the Gunpowder Plot

Left: A Protestant engraving illustrating that the gunpowder conspiracy could not be hidden from the all-seeing eyes of the Almighty

For two and a half centuries, until the Thanksgiving Act was abolished in 1859, Parliament adjourned every 5 November and processed across to Westminster Abbey or St Margaret's Church for this corporate act of worship. Though no longer compulsory by law, annual Bonfire Night festivities still continue unabated throughout Britain more than four centuries after Parliament was saved from destruction.

To ensure that the gunpowder atrocity was never repeated, the government became more diligent in protecting the royal family and parliamentarians at Westminster. Still today the vaults of the House of Lords are always searched before the State Opening of Parliament though this exercise has become part of the pageant. Since the beginning of the 20th century this duty has fallen to the Yeomen of the Guard (the monarch's ceremonial bodyguard), dressed in their traditional scarlet uniforms and carrying lanterns, lest Guy Fawkes return.

Above: St Margaret's Church, in the shadow of Westminster Abbey, has been known as the church of the House of Commons since the early 17th century. For 250 years MPs gathered here every 5 November to give thanks to God for deliverance from the Gunpowder Plot

Below: The Yeomen of the Guard prepare for their search before the Opening of Parliament

❸ Regicide

The relationship between Parliament and the Stuart kings was often strained. Yet even during the darkest days of the Civil War, few could believe the king would actually lose his head

'Idle heads and trouble makers' was the contemptuous verdict of James I upon the House of Commons. After the failure of the so-called 'Addled Parliament' of 1614, which was dissolved before a single statute was passed, he lamented to the Spanish ambassador: 'At their meetings nothing is heard but cries, shouts, and confusion. I am surprised that my ancestors should ever have permitted such an institution to come into existence.' Towards the end of his reign James prophesied that his son would 'live to have his bellyful of Parliaments'.

Defiance and dissolution

The young new king, Charles I, was initially hailed as 'Great Britain's Charlemagne', but his early Parliaments soon degenerated into mutual suspicion and recriminations. Money and religion were high on the agenda. The puritan majority in the House of Commons doubted his loyalty to Protestantism, especially after his marriage to a French Catholic princess, Henrietta Maria. At the Opening of Parliament in June 1625 the king had to scotch the rumour that he was not 'so true a keeper and maintainer of true religion as I profess', but the Commons still refused to grant him the customary tax-raising powers until he had listened to their religious grievances.

MPs fearlessly criticized royal policy, especially Charles' disastrous military expeditions against France and Spain, and his patronage of Arminian (anti-puritan) theologians like Richard Montague and William Laud. In May 1626 the Commons impeached the king's closest friend and chief adviser, George

Above: *Hubert le Sueur's bronze equestrian statue of Charles I was created in 1633 for the Earl of Portland. It is now erected at Trafalgar Square*

Facing page: *King Charles I, who tried to rule without Parliament*

Villiers (Duke of Buckingham) on charges of corruption and extortion. Sir John Eliot (MP for Newport) compared Buckingham to Sejanus, the ambitious confidant of the tyrannical Roman Emperor Tiberius. Two days into the duke's trial, Charles marched down from Whitehall to Westminster and imprisoned Eliot and Sir Dudley Digges, a flagrant breach of 'parliamentary privilege' (which guarantees MPs immunity from arrest while Parliament is in session). When this strategy did not work, the king simply dissolved their proceedings to protect his friend, reminding the Commons that 'Parliaments are altogether in my power'. Some feared he was pushing England towards absolute monarchy.

'Seditious vipers'

To finance his military exploits, Charles sold some of the crown jewels, melted down the royal plate and enforced loans from his subjects, but more was needed. At the Opening of his third Parliament in March 1628 he demanded immediate action from the MPs, which meant grants of money not 'tedious consultations'. The Commons voted him five subsidies when he promised to enforce anti-Catholic legislation, but they also passed a catalogue of grievances known as the Petition of Right. Quoting from *Magna Carta* and other medieval statutes, they declared the illegality of summary imprisonment, martial law, the billeting of troops in civilian homes, and the raising of loans

or taxes without Parliament's consent. A few months later the Duke of Buckingham was stabbed to death in Portsmouth by an aggrieved army officer who claimed to have been motivated by the Petition of Right.

In early 1629 the Commons endorsed the Elizabethan Settlement which had legally established Protestant reformed Christianity in England, and they called for a national day of prayer and fasting 'to Almighty God for the preservation of his true religion'. MPs condemned the 'subtle and pernicious spreading of the Arminian faction' and asked the king only to appoint bishops who were 'learned, pious and orthodox men'. When Charles tried to adjourn Parliament, the Commons defied him. The announcement was greeted with shouts of 'No! No!' Some MPs got up to leave but the doors were locked while Denzil Holles and Benjamin Valentine forcibly held the Speaker in his chair to allow debate to continue. As 'Black Rod' and other royal messengers tried to force their way into the chamber, the Commons passed Eliot's motion against Arminianism, Roman Catholicism and the payment of tonnage and poundage (excise duties). It was a turning point in the relationship between Parliament and the crown.

Many agreed that the Commons had gone too far. One puritan MP, Simonds D'Ewes, called it 'the most gloomy, sad and most dismal day for England that happened in five hundred years last past', blaming the

Above: The 'Pilgrim Fathers' depart from the Netherlands for New England in 1620 in search of religious freedom, while their pastor, John Robinson, exhorts them from the beach. It was painted by Charles West Cope for the Peers Corridor

debacle on 'diverse fiery spirits in the House of Commons'.

Charles dissolved Parliament for the third time in less than four years, chastising the 'undutiful and seditious' behaviour of a 'few vipers' in the House of Commons. Nine MPs were arrested and their ringleader, John Eliot, remained in the Tower of London until his death three years later. The king concluded that Parliament was more trouble than it was worth and he was now determined to rule without them, until the Commons 'shall come to a better understanding of us and themselves.'

Almost off the hinges'

It was not unusual for the king of England to rule without Parliament's advice. James I, for example, had called just one Parliament between 1610 and 1621. It was only his need for money which eventually forced Charles to summon MPs back to Westminster in April 1640, after

eleven years of 'personal rule'. He was at war again, this time in Scotland where he had provoked rebellion by trying to enforce the *Book of Common Prayer* upon the Scottish kirk. Soon the violence escalated from arguments about liturgy and episcopacy to a more fundamental question, as Charles put it, of 'whether we be their king or not'. The war needed finance which only Parliament could provide.

It was by no means clear how MPs would respond to the king's summons after such a long hiatus. As the Venetian ambassador observed, 'the long rusted gates of Parliament cannot be opened without difficulty.' John Finch,

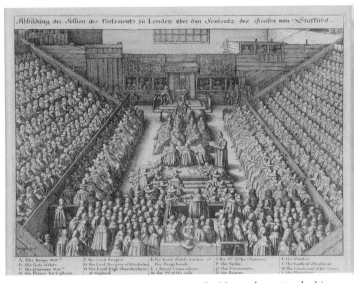

Above: *Etching from 1641 depicting the trial of the Earl of Strafford in Westminster Hall*

Lord Keeper of the Great Seal, told MPs bluntly that 'the king did not require their advice, but an immediate vote of supplies.' However, the Commons were not ready to submit meekly and they raised many of their old grievances. John Pym, a leading puritan MP, spoke passionately against economic and religious abuses, criticizing monopolies, illegal fines, and the tyranny of the church courts and the Star Chamber. In frustration Charles tried to bypass the Commons by persuading the Lords to vote taxes for his Scottish campaigns. Finally, in despair, he abruptly dissolved Parliament in May, after only three weeks, blaming the demise of this so-called 'Short Parliament' on 'the malicious cunning of some seditiously affected men.'

By November 1640 the king was back with his begging bowl and had no option but to recall MPs yet again. A Scottish army of 18,000 men had occupied the north-east of England and demanded a subsidy of £850 a day, otherwise they would march south. Charles also had his own troops to pay. Yet he was not in a conciliatory mood and blamed the Commons for the fact that the English government was 'all in pieces and, I must say, almost off the hinges.' Radicals and royalists in Parliament became increasingly polarized, and the Commons continued to flex its muscles by purging the king's key ministers. Thomas Wentworth (Earl of Strafford) and William Laud (Archbishop of Canterbury) were impeached and sent to the Tower, while other royal advisers fled to France or the Netherlands. Bishops in the House of Lords faced particular censure and 15,000 Londoners signed a petition demanding the abolition of the episcopate 'root and branch'. Charles conceded to the end of episcopacy in Scotland but promised to protect it in England as 'one of the fundamental institutions of this kingdom'.

Strafford's impeachment trial took place at Westminster Hall in March 1641. He faced thirty-one charges of corruption but defended himself so ably that the case collapsed. Therefore the Commons took a new line of attack. As a convenient way to bypass the common law, Pym introduced a Bill of Attainder which simply declared that Strafford was guilty and must be executed. In the past, attainder had been used to punish the crown's enemies, but now for the first time it was unleashed upon a royal friend. Mobs gathered at Westminster and attacked any MPs who opposed the bill as 'betrayers of their country'. It passed easily in the Commons, and the Lords also capitulated by 48 votes to 11. Charles had the power to block the bill and promised Strafford that 'upon the word of a king you shall not suffer in life, honour and fortune', signing himself 'your constant, faithful friend'. Yet, intimidated and fearful for his family's safety, Charles gave the bill his royal assent, a decision which tormented his conscience for the rest of his life. He begged the

Impeachment and attainder

The two key methods by which the Houses of Parliament conducted criminal proceedings against those in public office were impeachment and attainder.

The House of Commons could impeach an individual by presenting accusations to the House of Lords, where a trial would be held. The first record of this procedure was in 1376 when Sir William Latimer, chamberlain of the royal household, was accused of corruption. The last time it was employed in the Middle Ages was in 1459 against Sir Thomas Stanley, who refused to send his troops into the Battle of Blore Heath during the Wars of the Roses. Having fallen into disuse, impeachment was revived in 1621 to prosecute the Lord Chancellor, Sir Francis Bacon, and his associates for their part in a scandal over monopolies. There were a total of 54 cases between the 17th century and the last impeachment in 1806, of Viscount Melville for misappropriating public funds.

Attainder was a more brutal method, an Act of Parliament by which the Commons and the Lords simply declared an individual guilty of treason by majority vote and imposed the death sentence. It bypassed the need for a common law trial, and was often used in the late 15th and early 16th centuries as a convenient way to remove those who displeased the king, such as Cardinal Wolsey, Thomas Cromwell and Queen Katherine Howard. However, during the 1640s Parliament itself began to initiate bills of attainder to remove the king's friends. The last time an Act of Attainder was used as a substitute for a trial was against Sir John Fenwick in 1697 for his part in a Jacobite plot to assassinate William III.

Lords to commute the sentence to life imprisonment, but Strafford was beheaded at Tower Hill before a crowd of 100,000 people.

The king was rapidly losing control and tried to conciliate the Commons by giving ground. He assented to the abolition of tonnage and poundage, and the end of the notorious Court of the Star Chamber (thus stripping the Privy Council of its judicial powers). He also expelled Catholics from Henrietta Maria's court and allowed the execution of Jesuit priests. Yet Pym and his puritan allies continued to demand more reforms. In November 1641 Parliament passed the Grand Remonstrance, a lengthy recital of grievances against the king which claimed there was a 'malignant and pernicious design' to subvert England's ancient laws and reformed religion.

'All my birds have flown'
On 3 January 1642 Charles raised the stakes by publishing charges of high treason against six of his parliamentary critics: five in the Commons (John Pym, John Hampden, Arthur Hesilrige, Denzil Holles and William Strode) and one in the Lords (Viscount Mandeville). Mandeville offered to stand trial, but the others drew the king deeper into confrontation. The following afternoon they sat in the Commons as usual, enticing him to march down from Whitehall with a posse of soldiers. They then slipped away through a back door and escaped by

Above: C.W. Cope's portrayal of King Charles I's intrusion upon the House of Commons in January 1642. Speaker Lenthall, on his knees, defies the king's wishes

boat down the River Thames to hideouts in the City of London. A few minutes later, the king burst into the Commons Chamber and strode up to the Speaker's chair as the startled MPs stood in silence. He announced that parliamentary privilege did not apply in cases of treason and therefore the accused men must face justice.

As Charles looked around the room he could see that 'all my birds have flown', but asked Speaker Lenthall where they were. Lenthall fell to his knees and said, 'May it please your majesty, I have neither eyes to see, nor tongue to speak in this place, but as this House is pleased to direct me, whose servant I am here.' This was a remarkable declaration of allegiance to Parliament before the king. Charles was forced to retreat as cries of 'Privilege! Privilege!' rang forth.

The next day at the London Guildhall he was again met with chants of 'The privileges of Parliament!' from hostile aldermen and councillors. The monarch had lost control of his capital city. The five MPs returned to Westminster in triumph where the Commons proceeded to impeach the Attorney General, Sir Edward Herbert, who had announced the charges against them. On 10 January the royal family fled from Whitehall, first to Hampton Court and then to the security of Windsor Castle. This retreat from the seat of government had major political repercussions and was seen as a surrender of power. The next time Charles returned to the capital would be as a prisoner.

In the king's absence, the Commons seized control. Instead of 'Acts of Parliament' which

Below: A Victorian fresco in the Peers Corridor showing Charles I raising his standard at Nottingham, which signalled the start of the English Civil War

The Opening of Parliament

The Opening of Parliament is now one of the annual highlights in the Westminster calendar. It is a carefully choreographed ceremony with lavish pageantry, laden with historic symbolism. It demonstrates the sovereign's authority over Parliament, but also the carefully guarded independence of the House of Commons, rooted in their dramatic confrontation with Charles I in 1642.

Before the Queen's arrival, a member of the Commons (usually a government whip) is selected as a 'hostage' and taken to Buckingham Palace as an insurance policy in case the Commons are hostile, and is only released upon her safe return. The Queen is carried to Westminster Palace in a horse-drawn carriage, puts on her state robes and imperial state crown in the Royal Robing Room, and processes with her retinue through the Royal Gallery to her throne in the House of Lords. There the Queen's messenger, the Gentleman Usher of the Black Rod, is sent to summon the House of Commons. However, at

Right: The Gentleman Usher of the Black Rod bangs on the closed doors of the Commons Chamber

Below: Queen Elizabeth II and the Duke of Edinburgh at the State Opening of Parliament

the Commons Chamber the doors are ceremonially slammed in his face. He strikes the door three times with his staff (the Black Rod) demanding admittance, while MPs look through a grille in the door to make sure he has not brought a detachment of soldiers. The Commons then follow their Speaker to the House of Lords in a deliberately casual manner, to hear the Queen.

The Queen's Speech is prepared by the government, outlining their legislative agenda for the coming year. It traditionally ends with the words: 'My Lords and Members of the House of Commons, I pray that the blessing of Almighty God may rest upon your counsels.'

required royal assent, they passed 'ordinances' on their own authority. Soon they had taken charge of the army, the navy and the judiciary. As Charles prepared for war, Henrietta Maria sailed for the Netherlands to raise money for weapons by pawning the crown jewels. Parliament's first act of military defiance, in April 1642, was to refuse him access to the large arsenal at Hull. In the ensuing propaganda campaign the king spoke of 'war against Parliament', claiming that Westminster was dominated by a 'faction of malignant, schismatical and ambitious persons' who wanted to establish 'their own lawless arbitrary power and government.' In his formal declaration of war at Nottingham in August he maintained that he was fighting to protect Parliament from those MPs who had assaulted its 'dignity, privilege and freedom'.

Two rival Parliaments

Over the next four years England was torn apart by a devastating series of civil wars. The king chose Oxford as his new capital and refused to negotiate with the commissioners sent by the Commons. He absolved his subjects from obeying parliamentary edicts because Westminster had been taken over by radicals 'who have sacrificed the peace and prosperity of their country to their own pride, malice and ambition.'

In order to legitimize his own position, Charles summoned Parliament to Oxford in January 1644 where approximately 120 members of the Commons and thirty-five peers gathered in the great hall at Christ Church. They denounced their rivals at Westminster as traitors, but the king was eventually forced to acknowledge that the Oxford assembly was merely 'our mongrel Parliament' and he sent them home. The existence of two Parliaments, at Westminster and Oxford, both claiming legitimacy, made peace negotiations especially complicated.

Above: A parliamentary militia departs from London to battle with the royalists, from a painting in the Peers Corridor. One soldier sings from a hymn-book, while a puritan preacher urges them forward with sword aloft

At Westminster, reforms continued swiftly. Parliamentary ordinances abolished episcopacy, ordered the sale of bishops' palaces and lands, and replaced the *Book of Common Prayer* with the Westminster Directory (puritan guidelines for public worship). The Westminster Assembly of divines began to meet nearby at Westminster Abbey from 1643, constructing the Westminster Confession as a new doctrinal basis for the English church. The Committee for Scandalous Ministers removed any who resisted these parliamentary reforms and ejected almost a third of England's 9,000 parish clergy. Meanwhile Archbishop Laud was beheaded in January 1645, aged 72, after his impeachment trial before the House of Lords. Some of these measures were widely welcomed, though when Parliament banned Christmas there were outbreaks of rioting.

The turning point of the war, after a series of inconclusive battles, was Parliament's Self-Denying Ordinance in April 1645. This forced all members of the Commons and Lords to lay down their commissions in the army, thus separating military strategy from parliamentary squabbles. The ineffectual Earl of Essex was obliged to resign as Lord General and was replaced by Thomas Fairfax, who took charge of Parliament's New Model Army, a well trained and properly equipped fighting force. Within a year the king had been defeated. He fled Oxford in disguise under cover of darkness in April 1646, but was soon captured in Nottinghamshire by the Scottish army. The Scots handed him over into parliamentary custody in a deal worth £400,000, although Charles complained that he had been sold 'at too cheap a rate'.

An incorruptible crown

After the king's capture, the ideological gulf between the Houses of Parliament and the Army Council became

Above: New Palace Yard in 1647, with Westminster Hall on the left. The Clock Tower, an early predecessor of the Big Ben Clock Tower, was built by Edward III in the 1360s

Right: W.H. Fisk's dramatic portrayal of the trial of Charles I in Westminster Hall

Below: From the east wall of St Margaret's Church, Westminster, a small bust of Charles I looks defiantly across to the statue of his great nemesis, Oliver Cromwell

increasingly apparent. Even when the fighting was finished the army refused to disband, claiming that it was a better defence of the rights and liberties of English citizens than the Commons. Soon soldiers were demanding the impeachment of MPs, including Denzil Holles and ten other leading Presbyterians who were forced to flee. The key question was the fate of Charles who lay in prison at Carisbrooke Castle on the Isle of Wight. Parliament wanted to negotiate with him but army radicals, led by Oliver Cromwell and Henry Ireton, denounced the defeated monarch as a 'man of blood' who must be brought to account.

On 6 December 1648, Colonel Thomas Pride stood at the door of the House of Commons with a contingent of soldiers and a list of MPs drawn up by the army command. He arrested 45 members and excluded a further 186. This was a far worse breach of parliamentary privilege than the king's foiled attempt to arrest Pym and his allies six

years before. In protest, another 86 MPs withdrew, leaving a so-called 'Rump Parliament' with a membership of only about two hundred. One of the excluded MPs, Clement Walker, coined the name, lambasting the purged Commons as 'this fag end, this veritable Rump of a Parliament with corrupt maggots in it.' It was merely a puppet of the army, ready to do its bidding. The remaining MPs agreed that

Left: A mid-19th century depiction by an unknown artist of Charles I's trial, showing Westminster Hall with its magnificent hammerbeam roof

Below: A bronze tablet in the floor of Westminster Hall marks the spot where Charles I stood during his trial in January 1649

it was 'highly dishonourable and destructive of the peace of the kingdom' to continue negotiations with the king. Instead they chose 'to proceed by way of justice against him'.

Charles faced trial at Westminster Hall. The Rump Parliament established a high court under the presidency of John Bradshaw and named 135 judges, though only half obeyed the summons. They were an assortment of peers, aldermen, colonels and MPs, but the king joked that they were such an insignificant *mélange* that he only recognized eight of them. He refused to betray 'that duty I owe to God, and my country' by submitting to the

tyranny of an illegal tribunal. He warned that no citizen could be safe in a society where Parliament exercised naked power without reference to law. Nevertheless, Charles was sentenced to death as 'Tyrant, Traitor, Murderer, and Public Enemy to the good people.' As he was led from Westminster Hall under armed guard, some soldiers in the crowd spat at

This Tablet marks the spot where Charles Stuart King of England stood before the Court which sat pursuant to the ordinance for erecting a High Court of Justice for his trial which was read the first second & third time & passed by Parliament on the 4th January 1648–9.

The Court met on Saturday the 20th Monday the 22nd Tuesday the 23rd & on Saturday the 27th January 1648–9 when the sentence of Death was pronounced upon the King

Right:
Whitehall Palace, overlooking St James' Park, as it appeared in the 1680s before it was destroyed by fire

him and blew smoke in his face. Others cried, 'Execution!' and 'Justice!'

On Tuesday 30 January, the day of his execution, the king announced: 'This is my second marriage day … before night I hope to be espoused to my blessed Jesus. … I fear not death! Death is not terrible to me, bless my God, I am prepared.' At two o'clock that afternoon he was taken to the scaffold built in the street next to Whitehall Palace. It was draped in black, guarded by pikemen and surrounded by a vast crowd. Reiterating his defence of liberty and his defiance of arbitrary power, Charles proclaimed, 'I am a martyr to the people. … I die a Christian according to the profession of the Church of England, as I found it left me by my father. I have a good cause, and a gracious God on my side.' His chaplain, Bishop Juxon, reassured him that he would soon travel 'from earth to heaven; and there you will find, to your great joy, the prize you hasten to, a crown of glory.' The condemned man agreed, 'I go from a corruptible to an incorruptible crown.' He lay face-down on the floor, with his head on the block, and was despatched with one clean blow of the axe. A week later, Parliament voted to abolish the monarchy.

Above: All that remains of the vast Palace of Whitehall is the neoclassical Banqueting House, built by Inigo Jones in 1622. King Charles was beheaded here, on a temporary scaffold in the street

④ Rump to revolution

For centuries the English Parliament had consisted of Lords and Commons under the monarch's authority. Yet now the Commons ruled alone

The Levellers were a radical faction within the New Model Army who rose to prominence during the Putney Debates on constitutional reform, held at St Mary's Church, Putney near London in the autumn of 1647. They argued in their manifestoes, *The Agreements of the People*, for universal male suffrage, annual or biennial elections, and a fairer distribution of parliamentary seats. Although the Levellers were soon marginalized, their startling proposal for a unicameral (single chamber) Parliament came to fruition. In March 1649 the Rump Parliament abolished the monarchy as 'unnecessary, burdensome, and dangerous to the liberty, safety, and public interest of the people'. Next they got rid of the House of Lords as 'useless and dangerous to the people of England'. The nation's supreme authority was now 'the representatives of the people in Parliament'. England was no longer a kingdom but a commonwealth.

Barebone's Parliament

Despite its early reforming zeal, the Rump Parliament was reluctant to allow the religious radicalism which the army desired. The Toleration Act of 1650 abolished compulsory attendance at parish churches but did not go far enough. Cromwell finally lost patience, concluding that the Rump was no longer a 'Parliament for God's people'. In March 1653 he marched his musketeers to Westminster and after listening to the debate in the Commons, he proclaimed,

Above: *Marble bust of Oliver Cromwell in the Central Lobby*

Facing page: *Hamo Thornycroft's bronze statue of Oliver Cromwell, holding a sword and a Bible. It was installed outside Westminster Hall in 1899, despite fierce objections from Irish MPs because of Cromwell's repressive subjugation of Ireland in 1649*

'You have sat too long here for any good you have been doing. Depart, I say, and let us have done with you. In the name of God, go!' Speaker Lenthall was again in the chair and defied Cromwell as he had Charles I. He refused to budge, but was removed from his seat. Cromwell grabbed the Speaker's mace and gave it to his soldiers, exclaiming, 'What shall we do with this bauble? Here, take it away!' The Rump had ended with the same bullying tactics with which it began.

The new form of government was yet another failed experiment. The Nominated Assembly, as the name suggests, was not elected but nominated by local Christian congregations before being hand-picked by the Army Council. They wanted MPs who were 'fearing God and of approved fidelity and honesty'. Major-General Thomas Harrison championed the idea in the belief that the rule of the saints would precede the return of Christ, which was standard teaching amongst 'Fifth Monarchists', based on their interpretation of the Book of Daniel. The assembly was modelled on the council of seventy elders chosen by Moses to rule over Israel (Numbers 11:16), though

Cromwell doubled the size to 140. Vavasor Powell, another Fifth Monarchist and Welsh puritan, even suggested that common law be replaced by the Mosaic law.

The assembly was ridiculed by its opponents as 'Barebone's Parliament', named after one of its best known members, a London preacher called Praisegod Barebone (or Barbon). Cromwell hoped it would be a 'door to usher in things that God has promised', but within six months it collapsed amidst internal bickering. While the more radical members where praying early one morning, their rivals voted to dissolve the assembly and hand back power.

Above: *Francis Rous, puritan politician and Speaker during Barebone's Parliament, holding the Speaker's mace*

Cromwell's Protectorate

The next experiment in constitutional reform was the Instrument of Government, England's first ever written constitution, drafted by Major-General John Lambert. It created the position of Lord Protector, elected for life and with executive power to call and dissolve Parliament. Cromwell was chosen and thus became king in all but name. There were four hundred MPs at Westminster, to be elected triennially but scrutinized by the Council of State before they took their seats, to ensure they were 'persons of known integrity, fearing God and of good conversation'.

In Cromwell's opening speech to the first Protectorate Parliament in September 1654, he spoke of 'a door of hope opened to us by God'. Yet MPs refused to do as they were told or to ratify the bills put forward by the Council of State. They were soon campaigning for revision of the Instrument of Government, to give Parliament more authority. They wanted greater control over the militia and tried to reduce the size of the army, but without success. They also refused to sanction religious pluralism, enacting measures against 'blasphemy' and 'atheism'. The radical preacher John Biddle, was imprisoned by Parliament for denying the doctrine of the Trinity, and the army saw this as a direct assault upon liberty of conscience. In frustration, Cromwell dissolved their proceedings at the first opportunity, lamenting that

Above: *Cromwell addressing the second Protectorate Parliament in 1656*

'weeds and nettles, briers and thorns, have thriven under your shadow!'

The second Protectorate Parliament was equally acrimonious. It was summoned in September 1656 to provide financial backing for Cromwell's war against Spain and for the major-generals who were acting as military governors throughout the country. Yet many of the elected MPs remained hostile to the army's dominance. Over a hundred were purged by the Council of State for being 'ungodly', at which another fifty resigned in protest. Those who were left continued to resist Cromwell's injunctions for military and religious freedom. They refused to pass the Militia Bill and sought to restrain the spread of theological heterodoxy.

The most notorious case was that of James Nayler, a Quaker prophet who re-enacted Christ's

Left:
E.M. Ward's painting in the Commons Corridor, portraying General Monck's declaration for a 'free Parliament' which helped to usher in the restoration of the monarchy

triumphal entry into Jerusalem on Palm Sunday by riding into Bristol on horseback while his followers cast their garments on the ground and sang, 'Holy, Holy, Holy, Lord God of Hosts'. He was put on trial by Parliament, branded on his forehead with the letter B for blasphemy, and whipped through the streets of Westminster by the hangman.

Most controversially, MPs drafted a new constitution to replace the Instrument of Government, known as the Humble Petition and Advice, which represented a shift back towards old parliamentary traditions. It was calculated to weaken the army's influence and to restrain Cromwell by offering him the kingship. They believed that as monarch he would be stripped of the sweeping emergency powers he exercised as Lord Protector. Cromwell was tempted but eventually declined the invitation after fierce antagonism from the army leadership. He explained

that the monarchy had been 'providentially' destroyed like the city of Jericho in the Bible and that to rebuild it would bring curses on his head (Joshua 6:26). Nevertheless, many of the other suggestions in the Humble Petition and Advice were accepted. Cromwell was reinstalled as Lord Protector, with the right to choose his successor, provided that he ensured Parliament's 'ancient and undoubted liberties and privileges'. He was also allowed to nominate a revived second chamber, known as the 'Other House', a substitute for the abolished House of Lords.

Cromwell's second investiture as Lord Protector at Westminster Hall on 26 June 1657 took the form of a quasi-coronation. For the ceremony of 1653 he had been dressed in a plain black suit. Now he wore a purple robe lined with ermine. The coronation chair, used for the enthronement of every English monarch since Edward II in 1308, was brought across from Westminster Abbey. Cromwell was presented with a Bible, a sword and a golden sceptre as trumpets blared and heralds proclaimed his title. Within fifteen months he had died of pneumonia.

Monarchy restored

After Cromwell's death, England descended into anarchy. His son, Richard Cromwell, became Lord Protector and called fresh elections in January 1659, yet the civilian politicians and military leadership remained at loggerheads. The army forced Cromwell to dissolve his new Parliament and to recall the old Rump of 1653, which demanded the end of the Protectorate, forced Cromwell's resignation and declared all legislation passed over the previous six years to be illegal.

The power struggle between MPs and military commanders was only decided in Parliament's favour when General George Monck (commander of the army in Scotland) broke ranks and marched south with his troops. He reached the capital in February 1660 and brought back the Long Parliament (those MPs who sat at Westminster until Pride's Purge in December 1648) on condition that they dissolved themselves and called free elections. A strongly pro-royalist Convention Parliament came to power and the House of Lords was restored. In a remarkable turn of events, Parliament had come full circle.

Since the end of the Civil Wars, Prince Charles (son of the executed king and therefore heir to the throne) had lived in exile at Paris, Cologne, Bruges and Brussels plotting the restoration of the monarchy. Sensing an opportunity, he issued the Declaration of Breda laying down the terms on which he would accept the crown. He promised to grant a 'free Parliament', a 'free and general pardon' to all enemies except his father's

Right: *Ward's painting in the Commons Corridor, depicting the arrival of King Charles II on Dover beach in May 1660. The Union Jack is an anachronism, since it did not take this form until the Union of Britain and Ireland in 1801*

regicides, and religious toleration. In May he was proclaimed king by both Houses of Parliament and arrived triumphantly in London a few weeks later. Charles II's emphasis was on reconciliation as he sought to heal the wounds of the previous two decades, and Parliament was kept busy for many months unravelling the chaos from the Commonwealth and the Protectorate. All acts and ordinances passed unilaterally since 1642 without royal assent (about 1,200 in total) were declared null and void, and they began to legislate from scratch.

The Indemnity and Oblivion Act aimed to draw a line under the Interregnum. It restored all the property belonging to the crown and the church, but lands confiscated from royalists were not automatically forfeit by their new owners. All those who had fought against the monarchy were pardoned, except for a list of named individuals including the judges who signed Charles I's death warrant. Several were tried in Westminster Hall before being hung, drawn and quartered. Others were dug up from their graves in order to be punished. The corpses of Oliver Cromwell, Henry Ireton and

Downing Street

Downing Street, near the Houses of Parliament, was built in the 1680s by Sir George Downing, a diplomat and property developer who flourished under both Oliver Cromwell and Charles II. Raised in a puritan family, he trained at Harvard College in New England before serving as a chaplain in the New Model Army during the Civil War in Old England. He was a member of all three Protectorate Parliaments from 1654, but his political influence survived the restoration of the monarchy. Downing won a knighthood and a baronetcy for his service to the crown, which included the capture of three regicides who had sought sanctuary in the Netherlands. Just before his death in 1684 he erected fifteen townhouses in Westminster with views of St James' Park, designed by Sir Christopher Wren and named 'Downing Street'.

No. 10 Downing Street has been the official residence of the First Lord of the Treasury (the British Prime Minister) since 1735. The property next door, No. 11, has been the official residence of the Second Lord of the Treasury (the Chancellor of the Exchequer) since 1828. Most of the other original

Above: *The famous front door of No. 10 Downing Street in the 1960s*

houses on the street were demolished during the 19th century to make way for new government offices.

John Bradshaw were all exhumed from Westminster Abbey and hung in their shrouds at Tyburn on 30 January 1661 (the twelfth anniversary of the regicide). They were then decapitated and their heads impaled on pikes at Westminster Hall as a macabre reminder of their crimes. Cromwell's skull remained on display for more than twenty years until it was blown down in a gale. It became a collector's item in the 18th century and was finally reinterred in 1960 at Sidney Sussex College in Cambridge.

The Clarendon Code

Although Charles II promised in the Declaration of Breda to ensure 'liberty for tender consciences', his 'Cavalier Parliament' which sat from May 1661 had other ideas. They aimed to restore the Church of England to its former glory and authority, while stamping out religious nonconformity. They brought bishops back to the House of Lords and enacted a catalogue of repressive legislation known as the 'Clarendon Code', named after the new Lord Chancellor, Edward Hyde, first Earl of Clarendon.

The Corporation Act (1661) required all holders of civic office to renounce presbyterianism and take communion according to the rites of the Church of England. The Act of Uniformity (1662) required all clergymen to receive episcopal ordination and to give 'unfeigned assent and consent' to the *Book of Common Prayer*. As a result nearly one thousand ministers resigned as a matter

Above: Statue in St Stephen's Hall of the Earl of Clarendon, Lord Chancellor at the restoration of the monarchy, remembered for the repressive 'Clarendon Code'

of conscience and hundreds of others were forcibly ejected from their parishes. The Conventicle Act (1664) banned non-Anglican religious gatherings, and the Five Mile Act (1665) forbade all ejected preachers to go within five miles of any corporate town or the parish in which they used to minister.

This penal legislation led to the persecution and imprisonment of Nonconformists, many of whom fled across the Atlantic Ocean to New England where they could freely practise their Christian principles. The bubonic plague and the Great Fire which devastated London in 1665–66 were widely interpreted as divine judgement upon the government's harsh policies.

Below: The House of Commons at Prayer, a sketch from 1903 by André Castaigne

Parliamentary Prayers

While MPs were enforcing the *Book of Common Prayer* upon the church, they also established their own form of private prayer within the Houses of Parliament. They thought it natural to seek God's blessing on their proceedings each day, especially with national interests at stake. The first recorded prayers within the Commons Chamber date back to 1558, at the start of the reign of Queen Elizabeth I, when it was customary for the clerk of the House to read the Litany and then the Speaker to offer prayer, probably extempore. The Restoration Parliament in the 1660s appointed a Speaker's chaplain to lead daily prayers before business begins —a set pattern which is still followed today.

The short service starts with a recital of Psalm 67 ('God be merciful unto us, and bless us'), using Miles Coverdale's translation from the Great Bible of 1539, the first English Bible to be authorized by King Henry VIII. Then MPs turn to face their seats, with their backs to the Speaker and chaplain–a tradition from the time when they used to kneel on the benches in St Stephen's Chapel. The prayers include the Lord's Prayer, and petitions for the sovereign and the royal family, but the centrepiece of the short service is the Prayer for Parliament (see Box: The Prayer for Parliament). In the Commons prayers are led by the Speaker's chaplain and in the Lords by one of the bishops.

MPs may reserve a seat in the Commons by placing a 'Prayer Card' on it before the start of the day's business, provided they occupy that seat during prayers. This long-standing custom dates back at least to the 1640s, when it was resolved 'that neither book nor glove may give any man title or interest to any place, if they themselves be not at prayers.' Parliamentary prayers remain strictly private. The public and press galleries are not opened and television broadcasts do not begin until these daily devotions are completed. One 20th century Speaker called them 'our family prayers'.

The popish plot

In March 1672 Charles II revealed his well-known sympathy for Roman Catholicism by issuing a Declaration of Indulgence

The Prayer for Parliament

The Prayer for Parliament dates from the restoration of the monarchy in the 1660s. It is still used daily in the House of Lords and reads as follows:

'Almighty God, by whom alone kings reign, and princes decree justice; and from whom alone cometh all counsel, wisdom, and understanding; we thine unworthy servants, here gathered together in thy Name, do most humbly beseech thee to send down thy Heavenly Wisdom from above, to direct and guide us in all our consultations: And grant that we, having thy fear always before our eyes, and laying aside all private interests, prejudices, and partial affections, the result of all our counsels may be to the glory of thy blessed Name, the maintenance of true religion and justice, the safety, honour, and happiness of the Queen, the public wealth, peace, and tranquillity of the realm, and the uniting and knitting together of the hearts of all persons and estates within the same, in true Christian love and charity one towards another, through Jesus Christ our Lord and Saviour. Amen.'

Since the 1990s a shorter modern alternative has been adopted in the House of Commons:

'Lord, the God of righteousness and truth, grant to our Queen and her government, to Members of Parliament and all in positions of responsibility, the guidance of your Spirit. May they never lead the nation wrongly through love of power, desire to please, or unworthy ideals but laying aside all private interests and prejudices keep in mind their responsibility to seek to improve the condition of all mankind; so may your kingdom come and your name be hallowed. Amen.'

Right: Near the steps of the throne in the House of Lords is the Woolsack, the historic seat of the Lord Chancellor (and now of the Lord Speaker). It originated in the 14th century when wool was a symbol of England's prosperity

which suspended the parliamentary laws against Catholic recusants as well as the Clarendon Code against Protestant Nonconformists. His long-serving 'Cavalier Parliament' were horrified, arguing that the king had no right to suspend statute law. They responded

Right: The coronation banquet in Westminster Hall in 1685, to celebrate the accession of James II

by passing the Test Act which required everyone in civil or military office to denounce the doctrine of transubstantiation and to receive holy communion by the rites of the Church of England. This forced the immediate resignation of influential Catholics like Lord Clifford (the Lord Treasurer) and the king's own brother, James Duke of York (the Lord High Admiral). James had secretly converted four years earlier and provoked Parliament further by marrying Mary of Modena, a fifteen year-old Catholic princess.

Parliament's historic antipathy towards Catholicism was manipulated with disastrous consequences by Titus Oates, a bawdy and dissolute Anglican clergyman. In June 1678 he invented a story about a Jesuit conspiracy to assassinate the king and raise a rebellion, which he embroidered into a written 'Narrative'. It was sheer fantasy supported by forged letters, but the Privy Council were only too eager to believe his audacious claims. London was gripped by panic, Parliament declared a day of prayer and fasting for the king's protection, and the

Commons insisted that all non-resident Catholics be banished from within twenty miles of the capital. They passed a second Test Act, given royal assent in November 1678, which banned all Catholics from Parliament, a prohibition which remained in force for the next 150 years. The Commons also brought forward an Exclusion Bill to remove James from the line of succession to the throne, but this was voted down.

This mass hysteria resulted in innocent deaths. Between December 1678 and July 1681 twenty-four Catholics were executed, including nine Jesuits, many on the perjured evidence of Oates and his cronies. When common sense at last prevailed, Oates himself was put on trial at Westminster Hall in May 1685. Sir George Jeffreys (the Lord Chief Justice) lambasted 'the infirmity of his depraved mind, the blackness of his soul, the baseness of his actions' and denounced his crime as 'infinitely more odious than common murder'. Jeffreys lamented that perjury was not a capital offence, but Oates was pilloried outside Westminster Hall and whipped so soundly that he almost died.

The seven bishops

James II's accession was greeted in the summer of 1685 by a rebellion led by Charles II's illegitimate son, the Duke of Monmouth, who tried to wrest the throne from his Catholic uncle. The Protestant usurper was defeated at the Battle of Sedgemoor in Somerset and his following was crushed by the Bloody Assizes of Judge Jeffreys, at which hundreds were executed. The king used the emergency to consolidate his power. He commissioned 86 Catholics as officers in the army, in defiance of the Test Acts, and banned the bonfire celebrations on 5 November because of their anti-Catholic tone. When Parliament resisted, he dissolved it. Henry Compton was suspended as Bishop of London after telling the House of Lords that 'the laws of England were like the dykes of Holland, and universal Catholicism like the ocean–if the laws were once broken, inundation would soon follow.'

In April 1687 James issued his first Declaration of Indulgence for Liberty of Conscience, dispensing with the Test Acts and granting religious toleration. Some Protestants welcomed the move, notably the Quakers led by William Penn (to whom the king had recently granted vast tracts of land in North America, renamed Pennsylvania). However, many saw it as a blatant attempt to overthrow parliamentary law in favour of Catholicism. Next, the king tried to pack Parliament with his own candidates to ensure that the Test Acts would be permanently repealed. He amended borough charters in an attempt to rig the voting, and dismissed lords lieutenant who refused to cooperate with his plans.

James reissued his Declaration of Indulgence in April 1688 with an added demand that it be read in every parish church in the country. In response, Archbishop Sancroft of Canterbury summoned six fellow bishops to Lambeth Palace where they drew

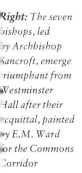

Right: The seven bishops, led by Archbishop Sancroft, emerge triumphant from Westminster Hall after their acquittal, painted by E.M. Ward for the Commons Corridor

up a petition asserting that it was illegal for the king to dispense with parliamentary statutes and that they would have nothing to do with the distribution of his Declaration in their dioceses. Five more bishops added their names over the next fortnight, but it was the first seven who bore the brunt of royal wrath. They rowed across the River Thames from Lambeth to Whitehall (minus Sancroft) to challenge James. Furious with rage, he called it 'a standard of rebellion', but Bishop Ken of Bath and Wells responded, 'We are bound to fear God and honour the king. We desire to do both. We will honour you; we must fear God.' Somehow the petition was leaked and within two hours it was being hawked through the streets of London.

The seven bishops were imprisoned at the Tower of London and then put on trial in Westminster Hall. They were charged with having written a 'false, feigned, malicious, pernicious and seditious libel' and then of publishing it to the world. Yet their defence lawyers argued persuasively that it was the king himself who had broken the law. The jury's verdict of 'Not Guilty' was greeted with jubilation throughout the capital and the bishops were hailed as national heroes.

The Coronation Service

William and Mary's coronation service deliberately followed the traditional format, in order to emphasize their legitimacy within the British monarchy. They retained the ancient coronation symbols like spurs and sword, orb and sceptre. William and Mary were anointed with oil like the kings of Israel and Judah in the Old Testament, and kissed the Bible as their predecessors had done. Yet there were also two significant innovations. First, the Bible was given extra prominence. It was symbolically presented to the new monarchs as 'the most valuable thing that this world affords' and Bishop Compton exhorted them to make it 'the rule of your whole government and life'. Second, the coronation oath was changed so that William and Mary now promised to the utmost of their power to 'maintain the laws of God, the true profession of the gospel, and the protestant reformed religion established by law'. These innovations helped to consolidate Britain's identity as a Protestant nation and have been retained in every coronation service since 1689.

Above: *King William III, in the Royal Gallery*

Above: The Lords and Commons offer the British crown to William and Mary, painted in the 1860s by E.M. Ward for the Commons Corridor

The Glorious Revolution

The acquittal of the seven bishops was a propaganda disaster for James II and demonstrated the strength of popular opinion against him. That very evening, 30 June 1688, seven peers (including Bishop Compton) secretly invited the king's Protestant son-in-law, William of Orange, to invade England because 'nineteen parts of twenty of the people are desirous of a change'. William landed at Torbay in Devon on 5 November, an auspicious date. He proclaimed that he had arrived to protect the freedom of Parliament and the church, but James called him 'worse than Cromwell' and denounced the invasion as unchristian. The king's authority evaporated and he was soon deserted by the army, the navy and many of the leading aristocracy. Faced by growing anarchy, he promised to call a free Parliament for January 1689, but it was too late so he fled to France.

It was impossible to call fresh parliamentary elections because the borough charters had become so confused by James' meddling. Therefore William summoned all MPs who had sat at Westminster during the reign of Charles II. They declared that James had abdicated the throne by his absence and, after some vacillation, they invited William and Mary to become joint sovereigns instead. Archbishop Sancroft felt honour-bound by his oaths of allegiance to James and was therefore deprived of his office, along with several episcopal colleagues (the start of the non-juror tradition). However, Bishop Compton had

*Left: The House of
Commons, formerly St
Stephen's Chapel, in the
early 18th century. The
galleries were added by
Sir Christopher Wren*

*Right: Mural in St
Stephen's Hall, showing
Queen Anne at St James'
Palace receiving the
articles of agreement
for the union of the
Parliaments of England
and Scotland in July
1707*

no such crisis of conscience and it
was he who crowned William and
Mary at Westminster Abbey in
April 1689.

One of the first acts of their
new Parliament was to pass
the Bill of Rights which placed
important limits on royal
authority and gave shape to this
new constitutional monarchy.
It was designed to end royal
despotism once and for all, and
was seen by some as a modern
version of *Magna Carta*.
Parliament was guaranteed
freedom of speech in its debates
without fear of prosecution,
and given control of taxation
and deployment of the army in
peacetime. The sovereign was
banned from interference in
parliamentary elections and the
law courts, while MPs were given
the right to petition the crown.
The Bill of Rights also banned
Roman Catholics from the throne
and made the new Protestant
coronation oath a statutory
obligation.

Occasional conformity

Soon after the Glorious
Revolution, Parliament passed
the Toleration Act granting
Protestant Nonconformists the
freedom to worship in public for
the first time. Nevertheless they
were still theoretically excluded
from political life since the
Corporation
Act and Test
Acts remained
in force,
requiring
everyone in
civil office to
attend holy
communion
once a year
according to
the rites of
the Church
of England.

*Right: Statue
of Queen Anne,
from the Royal
Gallery*

Some Nonconformists submitted to this annual test while still remaining members of their own denominations, but their habit of 'occasional conformity' seemed to contradict the spirit of the law, if not the letter.

Daniel Defoe, a Nonconformist businessman and author, is best remembered for novels such as *Robinson Crusoe* (1719) and *Moll Flanders* (1722). He was also a campaigner for religious liberty but chastised his fellow Nonconformists for trying to dodge the Test and Corporation Acts, rebuking them for 'playing Bo-peep with God Almighty' for the sake of political office. High church Anglicans were also quick to accuse occasional conformists of 'the lowest and basest of all hypocrisies' and mocked their willingness to adopt 'any or no religion' rather than lose preferment. During Queen Anne's reign there were several attempts to close the loophole in the law and restrict Nonconformists even further. In 1711 the Act for Preserving the Protestant Religion, known as

the Occasional Conformity Act, imposed fines on all office holders who attended Nonconformist meetings. This was followed in 1714 by the Schism Act which banned Nonconformists from teaching in schools or acting as tutors. But these acts were repealed in 1719 by the Whig government who came into the ascendancy under the Hanoverian kings.

A new campaigning organization, the Protestant Dissenting Deputies, was established in 1732 with two representatives from every Nonconformist congregation within ten miles of London. For a century they lobbied Parliament for the removal of civil disabilities, but it took until April 1828 for the Test and Corporation Acts to be repealed. The Cavalier Parliament had cast a long shadow over Westminster, but at long last Nonconformists were given back their voice within national politics.

⑤ Strike off the shackles

Parliament prided itself as the champion of liberty, but was slow to promote emancipation for African slaves and Irish Catholics. Both these hard fought campaigns reached a climax in the early 19th century

Roman Catholics had long been excluded from political life and faced a vast array of penal legislation dating back to the Reformation. They were banned from sitting in Parliament by the second Test Act in 1678 and then even banned from voting in elections by the Act for the Security of the Crown in 1696. The abortive Jacobite Rebellions led to a further backlash when conspirators tried to remove the Protestant German-speaking Hanoverians from the throne and bring back the Catholic English-speaking Stuart dynasty. At Westminster, several peers were impeached and executed, including Lord Lovat in 1745, the last person to be publicly beheaded in Britain.

In order to recruit Catholics for the British army to help quell the American Revolution (the War of Independence), Lord North's government passed the Catholic Relief Act in June 1778, the first pro-Catholic legislation since the reign of Mary Tudor. Although largely symbolic, it allowed Catholics to purchase and inherit property and to teach in schools; it also abolished rewards for informers against Catholic priests. Other disabilities remained firmly in place, including complete exclusion from public life, but Protestants were nevertheless alarmed at this apparent threat to the British constitution. John Wesley, the Methodist preacher, spoke out stridently against the Act, reminding his congregation of the 'raging fires of Smithfield',

Above: The official record of parliamentary debates is known today as 'Hansard', named after Luke Hansard, printer of the House of Commons journals from 1774 to 1828

Facing page: William Wilberforce, leader of the parliamentary campaign to abolish slavery, painted by George Richmond

Above: New Palace Yard in the 1790s, with Westminster Hall in the centre

where many evangelicals were burned during the Reformation. The Protestant Association was founded in 1779 to campaign for the Act's repeal, under the presidency of a young Scottish MP, Lord George Gordon.

The Gordon Riots

On Friday, 2 March 1780 Gordon led a deputation to the House of Commons to present the government with a 'monster petition' signed by nearly 120,000 people. His supporters gathered at St George's Fields south of the river (where Waterloo Station now stands) and marched to Parliament Square carrying banners emblazoned with 'No Popery!' and shouting that they would 'rather perish in the streets than endure a popish government'. They numbered 50,000 and their ranks were soon swelled by others (including prostitutes, pickpockets and street gangs) who had no interest in religious or constitutional questions.

When MPs began to arrive, the demonstration turned nasty. Some had their carriages smashed, others were kicked and beaten, and pelted with mud and excrement. Lord Ashburnham was carried into the House of Lords over the heads of the mob, barely conscious. Welbore Ellis (MP for Weymouth) was hit in the face with a whip and then chased through the streets, running for his life. Many of the original petitioners went home in dismay and withdrew their support from the Protestant Association, but a crowd of more than 10,000 continued to beat at the doors of Parliament, shouting 'Repeal! Repeal!' and 'Gordon! Gordon!' In the House of Commons, Gordon dumped his enormous petition (a giant roll of parchment) on the floor and demanded its immediate consideration. Yet after six hours of debate, as the violence flared outside, only seven MPs voted with him.

The rioters were eventually dispersed from Parliament Square by the Foot Guards and Horse Guards, but rampaged through the streets of the capital. For the next week chaos ensued. Houses were looted, prisons and distilleries were destroyed. Many homes were deliberately targeted, including those of Lord Mansfield (the Lord Chief Justice) and the Archbishop of York. Rioters laid siege to the Bank of England, and it was rumoured that Lord North had been lynched at Downing Street, the king and queen murdered, and the Houses of Parliament burned down. Gordon and the Protestant Association publicly dissociated themselves from the carnage, but the government was unable to re-establish order. The Riot Act of 1713 was read at several locations before the militia fired at the crowd. Lord North talked of imposing martial law and Parliament debated the need for a professional police force. Not until 1829 did Sir Robert Peel's Metropolitan Police Act put 'Bobbies' on the streets of London.

By the time the trouble was quelled many lay dead. The government admitted that 285 people had been killed by the militia, but perhaps as many as 850 lost their lives in the violence. At least twenty-one were hung in the reprisals that followed. Gordon was put on trial for treason at Westminster Hall,

Below: An early 19th century watercolour by G.F. Robson of Westminster, as seen from Westminster Bridge

Above: New Palace Yard in the early 19th century, with the abbey in the background

accused of raising a rebellion 'not having the fear of God before his eyes but being seduced by the instigation of the devil.' Some conspiracy theorists claimed he was deployed by American revolutionaries, perhaps paid with French money via Benjamin Franklin. Lord Mansfield told the prisoner that Parliament would never be intimidated by mob violence: 'Nothing can be so dishonourable to government, as to be forced to make, or to repeal, by an armed multitude, any law; from that moment there is an end of all legislative authority.' Although Gordon was acquitted, he was dismissed from Parliament. He later converted to Judaism, taking the name Israel Abraham George Gordon, and died of typhoid fever in Newgate gaol, having been imprisoned for libel and sedition.

Traffic in flesh and blood

The campaign for Catholic emancipation was temporarily drowned out at the end of the 18th century by a new protest movement seeking freedom for African slaves. Britain, as a global superpower with a dominant navy, was at the forefront of the slave trade between West Africa and the plantations of the West Indies and North America. In total, approximately three million slaves were transported in British ships.

As the abolitionist movement began to gather momentum on both sides of the Atlantic, a Committee for the Abolition of the Slave Trade was founded in London in May 1787 by Granville Sharp, Thomas Clarkson and a small group of English Quakers, who saw it as the first step towards the end of slavery itself. They needed someone inside the Houses of Parliament to champion the cause and so approached William Wilberforce, the 28 year-old MP for Yorkshire who had recently experienced evangelical conversion. He gladly accepted the challenge as a divine calling, seeking to combine Christian principles with political action. Wilberforce was optimistic that victory would soon be won against this 'horrid traffic in flesh and blood', not anticipating a protracted parliamentary struggle.

The abolitionist agenda won the support of the young Prime Minister, William Pitt, as well as the leaders of the Whig opposition, Charles James Fox and Edmund Burke. In May 1788 Pitt told the Commons that the slave trade was 'shocking to humanity' and 'the greatest dishonour on the British nation'. Yet abolition did not receive official government backing because the cabinet was split. Some argued that the slave trade was essential for the British economy, others that it was sanctioned by the Bible. Every parliamentary tactic was employed to disrupt and delay emancipation.

The greatest hindrance to Wilberforce's campaign were the political developments on the other side of the English Channel. The violent anarchy unleashed by the French Revolution, with its cry of 'liberty' and 'equality', provoked a conservative reaction at Westminster where MPs were eager to uphold monarchy, church and status quo. After Wilberforce lost his first major debate on abolition, in April 1791, he proclaimed, 'Never, never, will we desist till we have wiped away this scandal from the Christian name ... and extinguished every trace

of this bloody traffic ... a disgrace and dishonour to this country.' Every year he brought forward a similar motion, only to be constantly defeated. John Newton (a former slave trader and author of many evangelical hymns, such as *Amazing Grace*) urged Wilberforce to persist, writing in July 1796 that 'you are not only a representative for Yorkshire,

Above: *Statues in St Stephen's Hall of the great parliamentary rivals, William Pitt the Younger and Charles James Fox*

Above: The Buxton Memorial in Victoria Tower Gardens, built to commemorate the successful campaign to abolish slavery in British dominions

Minister, Lord Grenville, headed a coalition government known as 'The Ministry of All The Talents' who threw their weight behind abolition in a way Pitt's cabinet had never done. First they pushed through a Slave Importation Bill which banned the sale of slaves to French colonies in the West Indies and had the effect of destroying three quarters of the British slave trade at one stroke. Next they introduced a Slave Trade Abolition Bill in February 1807, to ban the sale of slaves outright. It passed in the Lords (where the Prime Minister sat) by 100 votes to 34, before being carried in the Commons by 283 votes to 16. After two decades of fierce and protracted parliamentary struggle, the final hurdle was overcome with surprising ease. Bishop Porteus of London, who had championed the cause in the House of Lords, believed it would 'reflect immortal honour on the British Parliament, the British nation and all the illustrious men who were the principal promoters of it.' Grenville welcomed it as the 'most glorious measure that had ever been adopted by any legislative body in the world.'

you have the far greater honour of being a representative for the Lord, in a place where many know him not.' Meanwhile the slave trade continued to boom. In the last decade of the 18th century British ships carried more than 400,000 slaves from Africa to the Americas, breaking all previous records.

An 'immortal honour'

Pitt's death in January 1806, aged only 46, and the escalation of the war with France marked a turning point in the anti-slavery campaign. The new Prime

Wilberforce was quick to acknowledge that he was 'only one among many fellow labourers', but plaudits were heaped upon him for the success of the long emancipation campaign. In the Lords, the Prime Minister proclaimed that Wilberforce's memory would be 'blessed by millions as yet unborn'. In the Commons, Sir John Doyle praised his 'indefatigable zeal … which washed out this foul stain from the pure ermine of the national character.' Sir Samuel Romilly (the Attorney General) contrasted him with Napoleon: the French tyrant had slaughtered many thousands, but the MP for Yorkshire had saved the lives of millions. In response, the Commons stood to applaud (an almost unique occurrence in parliamentary history) while Wilberforce sat with tears streaming down his face.

It was to be another generation, however, before slavery itself was abolished in British dominions. Wilberforce played a less prominent role in the Commons from the 1810s and resigned his seat in February 1825,

aged 65. He was increasingly frail and described himself as 'a bee which has lost its sting'. His mantle was picked up by Thomas Fowell Buxton (MP for Weymouth), another evangelical politician who championed many humanitarian causes in Parliament. The Anti-Slavery Society was founded in 1823 with Buxton as vice-president to push for outright abolition. The Jamaican slave rebellion of 1831 helped to swing government opinion, and the Abolition of Slavery Act finally received royal assent in August 1833. It brought emancipation for 700,000 African slaves in the West Indies, though they were required to serve a four year apprenticeship

The Clapham Sect

William Wilberforce was part of a circle of wealthy evangelical Christians associated with the village of Clapham in Surrey (soon a growing London suburb). They shared many family connections and a desire to see British society transformed by the Christian message, so were nicknamed the 'Clapham Sect'. The circle included a number of politicians, such as Henry Thornton, Charles Grant, Edward Eliot, James Stephen and Thomas Babington. They made a wide-ranging contribution to public life, particularly in philanthropic concerns

pursued in Parliament. The abolition of slavery was the Clapham Sect's greatest achievement, but they also campaigned energetically to improve education for children, care of the sick and destitute, prison reform, better conditions for factory workers, and the end of capital punishment for all but the most serious crimes.

The Clapham Sect's most controversial initiative was the Society for the Suppression of Vice, established in 1801. Wilberforce wrote in his diary in 1787 that 'God Almighty has set before me two great objects, the suppression of the slave trade and the reformation

of manners.' He believed that parliamentary legislation should promote both public and private morality. The Society campaigned against social ills such as pornography, brothels, drunkenness, duelling, brutal sports (like bear-baiting and cockfighting), gambling and the national lottery. However, Sydney Smith, the radical political commentator, complained in the *Edinburgh Review* in 1809 that these evangelical politicians only wanted to suppress 'the vices of persons whose income does not exceed £500 per annum', while leaving the sins of the aristocracy largely unchallenged.

under their former masters. In a parliamentary compromise, the planters were voted twenty million pounds in compensation for their loss of property, while the slaves received nothing in compensation for their loss of freedom.

Assassination

In October 1809 Spencer Perceval, a firm advocate of the abolition of slavery, became the new Prime Minister. Like Wilberforce he was marked out in Parliament by his religious convictions, having converted to evangelical Christianity as an undergraduate in Cambridge in the 1780s, and was an energetic supporter of philanthropic causes. Perceval's brief premiership was troubled by a number of political crises, not least the mental illness of King George III whose powers were devolved by Act of Parliament in February 1811 to his son as Prince Regent (the future George IV). Meanwhile social unrest spread through the midlands and north of England as skilled workers in the wool and cotton industries smashed mechanized looms, an act of sabotage which Perceval's government made a capital offence under the Frame Breaking Act. So-called 'Luddites' were executed in Lancashire and Yorkshire, while others were transported to Australia.

On the afternoon of Monday 11 May 1812, Perceval walked briskly from Downing Street to the House of Commons, late for a debate about the government's response to the ongoing Napoleonic Wars. As he arrived

Above: *Perceval is shot by John Bellingham in the lobby of the House of Commons, from a contemporary print*

Below: *Bellingham stands trial at the Old Bailey*

JOHN BELLINGHAM.
Taken at the Sefsions House
Old Bailey May 15-1812.

in the Commons lobby at about 5.15 pm he was approached by a stranger who pulled out a pistol and shot him through the heart. Perceval staggered forward, said 'I am murdered!' and fell dead. As the news spread, there was pandemonium in the House. Was this the start of an organized revolution? The Foot Guards and Horse Guards were called out on to the streets. Parliament was adjourned, and the doors of the Palace of Westminster were locked and guarded. Some feared a plot by Luddites or Roman Catholics. Rumours spread through London that the assassin was the radical MP Sir Francis Burdett, and a mob gathered outside Parliament to cheer him. The murder was celebrated in cities like Nottingham, Leicester and Sheffield with bonfires and riots, while placards were pasted upon the House of Commons proclaiming that 'Mr Perceval's ribs were only fit to broil the Regent's heart on'.

It soon became apparent that the assassin was not a revolutionary, but a disillusioned individual working alone. His name was John Bellingham, an insurance broker from Liverpool. He had spent four years in rat-infested prisons in Russia after a business relationship turned sour, and he held a grudge against the British government for refusing to help him. Bellingham's fight for justice, and for financial compensation, became an obsession. He petitioned the Foreign Secretary, the Home Secretary, the Treasury, the Privy Council, the Prince Regent, and the Prime Minister, and he sent a circular to every MP in the Commons, all without success. So as a last resort he shot the Prime Minister, complaining of 'want of redress of grievances'.

Above: *Spencer Perceval, the evangelical Prime Minister*

Perceval was only 49 years old and left behind a young widow and twelve children. His body was laid out at 10 Downing Street where Jane Perceval knelt with her sons and daughters and prayed for the murderer to be forgiven. This act of grace caused Wilberforce to exclaim in his diary: 'Oh wonderful power of Christianity!' The Commons voted to grant Mrs Perceval an annuity of £2,000 per year and a lump sum of £50,000 to support

Above: *Westminster Hall in the mid-18th century, showing the law courts and rows of shops*

his orphaned children. They also agreed to erect a public monument in Westminster Abbey, though some MPs doubted that Perceval's modest political legacy deserved such an honour.

British justice was swift in the 19th century and Bellingham was tried at the Old Bailey only four days after the murder. There was not enough time for his counsel to prepare a defence and, despite suggestions that the prisoner was insane, the jury took only fourteen minutes to return a 'Guilty' verdict. The *Times* newspaper, alluding to the Bible's judgment upon murder (Genesis 9:6), proclaimed, 'If ever there was one who for shedding man's blood

deserved that his blood should be shed, this is that person.' Two of Perceval's friends, James Stephen (anti-slavery campaigner and MP for East Grinstead) and Daniel Wilson (future Bishop of Calcutta), visited the condemned man in his cell, seeking to lead him to 'true repentance' and evangelical faith in Jesus Christ, but without success. Bellingham was hung at Newgate prison on 18 May, a week after the murder, and then his body was publicly dissected at St Bartholomew's Hospital. Later generations were horrified at the haste with which he was rushed to execution and in 1871 the legal reformer, Lord Brougham, called his trial 'the greatest disgrace to English justice'.

Spencer Perceval is the only British Prime Minister ever to be assassinated, though there have been other attempts. In January 1843 a Scottish political radical, Daniel McNaughten, plotted to kill Sir Robert Peel. Yet he mistook Edward Drummond, the Prime Minister's private secretary, for Peel himself and shot him in the back as he was walking towards Downing Street. McNaughten was acquitted of murder on the grounds of insanity which provoked a public outcry and forced the House of Lords to draw up a legal definition of criminal responsibility, the so-called 'McNaughten Rules'. The assassin spent the rest of his life in lunatic asylums, though there is evidence that he feigned insanity to avoid the hangman's noose.

The Liberator

The question of civil disabilities suffered by Roman Catholics was forced back on to the political agenda by the Union of Britain and Ireland in 1801 when the Dublin Parliament was merged with that at Westminster. As lawless violence swept through Ireland, nurtured by poverty and historic grievances, Parliament could no longer afford to ignore the issue, although numerous royal commissions and select committees failed to find a solution. Many at Westminster were alarmed at the prospect of an Irish rebellion but also believed that the presence of Catholics in the Commons would undermine Britain's national Protestant identity. For example, John Leslie Foster (MP for County Louth) believed that 'If every sect or religion be admitted to an equal share of government, the Protestant religion will cease to become what we have hitherto considered it–an essential portion of our glorious constitution.'

In 1823 two Dublin barristers, Richard Lalor Sheil and Daniel O'Connell, founded the Catholic Association to campaign for political equality. O'Connell, nicknamed 'The Liberator', soon rose to pre-eminence in the struggle for Catholic rights. In July 1828 he stood for election

Above: *Daniel O'Connell, Catholic emancipator*

in County Clare against William Vesey-Fitzgerald, a member of the Duke of Wellington's cabinet, and won a resounding victory in the poll. Yet he could not take up his seat at Westminster because he would 'rather be torn limb from limb' than make the anti-Catholic oaths required of all MPs. Addressing his supporters a few days later in Dublin, he proclaimed, 'I ask, what is to be done with Ireland? What is to be done with the Catholics? One of two things. They must either crush us or conciliate us. There is no going on as we are.' In an emotive speech he outlined the many ways in which England had oppressed Ireland over the centuries, but announced, 'all shall be pardoned, forgiven, forgotten, upon giving us emancipation, unconditional, unqualified, free and unshackled.'

Almost by accident, the Catholic Association had stumbled upon a new political strategy which blew the emancipation question wide open. Here, for the first time, was a Roman Catholic legally and constitutionally elected to the Westminster Parliament. There was nothing the government could do to stop it. Nor could they prevent Catholics winning every seat in Ireland over the next few years, if the electorate so chose. If these men were barred from the House of Commons, civil unrest would be inevitable. Soon the Union would unravel if those excluded from Westminster established themselves as an independent Parliament in Dublin, without legal authority but with a mandate from the people. Looking back two decades later, Robert Peel argued that the County Clare election was the key turning point in the emancipation campaign. It forced Wellington's government to face up to political realities.

Honour and betrayal

At the Opening of Parliament in February 1829, after the long summer recess, the Prime Minister made it clear that the government had now abandoned its neutrality on Roman Catholic emancipation. Wellington took up the campaign in the House of Lords, as did his deputy, Robert Peel, in the House of Commons. Both men were known to have argued against emancipation in the past and their change of heart brought accusations of betrayal from their erstwhile allies in the Tory party. Indeed Peel had been elected in 1818 to his prestigious seat as MP for Oxford University

Above: The Duke of Wellington, hero of the Battle of Waterloo and Prime Minister 1828-30

precisely because he came forward as a champion of Protestantism.

As a matter of personal honour, Peel now resigned his seat and stood for re-election, though his friend, J.W. Croker, warned that it would set a dangerous precedent of MPs being bound by promises to the electorate! Oxford graduates from all over Britain travelled to the university to cast their votes and Peel was trounced in the poll by Sir Robert Inglis, an evangelical friend of Wilberforce and the Clapham Sect. The Prime Minister's righthand man therefore had to find a 'rotten borough' (with a tiny electorate) to give him a place back in the Commons.

Despite widespread opposition, Wellington and Peel pushed ahead with their plans. They devised a complex new oath for Catholic MPs which required them to affirm loyalty to the Hanoverian succession, repudiate the pope's right to exercise civil jurisdiction in Britain, and promise not to undermine the Protestant establishment. It was also agreed that Catholics would still be excluded from some public offices, in particular those of Regent, Lord Chancellor, and Lord Lieutenant of Ireland. There was no bar, however, on the Prime Minister being a Catholic since in theory that honorary title can be attached to any government office.

In the House of Lords, the Earl of Winchilsea claimed that

Above: Statue in Parliament Square of Sir Robert Peel, who served twice as Prime Minister between 1834 and 1846

Wellington's conduct was 'more arbitrary and dictatorial than any act of any former Prime Minister.' In the pages of the *Standard* newspaper he went further, suggesting that Wellington merely pretended to be a zealous Protestant so that he could better promote 'his insidious designs, for the infringement of our liberties, and the introduction of popery into every department of the state.' The duke was stung by this assault on his personal integrity and when Winchilsea refused to apologize, he challenged his slanderer to a duel. The two men faced each other at Battersea Fields at dawn on 21 March 1829, with pistols drawn. Wellington deliberately fired at Winchilsea's

Above: Sir Richard Westmacott's statue in Parliament Square of Prime Minister George Canning, who died in August 1827 after only 119 days in office. It remains the shortest total period in office of any Prime Minister

legs, but missed and hit his coat. Then Winchilsea raised his gun and fired in the air. Although honour was preserved on all sides, they were ridiculed for allowing their quarrel to degenerate to such extremes.

A bloodless revolution

King George IV was deeply reluctant to grant political equality to Roman Catholics because he believed it was contrary to his coronation oath to uphold 'the protestant reformed religion as by law established'. At the time of his enthronement in 1821 he had warned, 'Remember, once I take that oath, I am for ever a Protestant king, a Protestant

---

Parliamentary duels

The clash between Wellington and Winchilsea at Battersea Fields in 1829 was only the latest in a series of duels fought between Members of Parliament. When disputes could not be settled by oratory or argument on the floor of the Commons or the Lords, they were sometimes decided by pistols at dawn. In November 1763 the radical pamphleteer and libertine, John Wilkes, fought a duel against his fellow MP, Samuel Martin, who had insulted him as 'a cowardly and malignant scoundrel' during a debate in the Commons. Likewise

Charles James Fox was called to fight William Adam at Hyde Park in November 1779, after Fox had ridiculed him for supporting Lord North's government.

William Wilberforce urged that duelling be outlawed as part of his campaign for the reformation of British morals. In his best-selling book, *A Practical View* (1797), he denounced the practice as 'the disgrace of a Christian society'. Wilberforce was particularly alarmed when his friend, the younger William Pitt, agreed to a duel in 1798 at the height of the war against France. The Prime Minister had accused his

fellow MP George Tierney of trying to 'obstruct the defence of the country', and refused to retract his remark when called upon to do so by the Speaker. Therefore Pitt and Tierney duelled at Putney Heath on 27 May (Pentecost Sunday) and although neither were injured, Pitt was chastised for risking his life in the midst of a national crisis. In another cause célèbre, rival cabinet ministers Canning and Castlereagh duelled on Putney Heath in September 1809. Canning was wounded and both were forced to resign from the government as the Duke of Portland's ministry ended in debacle.

upholder, a Protestant adherent.' He was determined to veto any bill for emancipation and talked of dissolving Parliament or even of abdication. No monarch had vetoed a parliamentary bill since Queen Anne in 1708, so such a step would have provoked a constitutional crisis. Finally the king's intransigence gave way when Wellington and Peel threatened to resign. He gave his royal assent on 13 April 1829,

deliberately snubbed O'Connell by ensuring that the Act was not retrospective. When he appeared before a crowded House of Commons to take his seat, he was refused the right to take the new oath. Therefore, the first Catholic MP since the Glorious Revolution was not O'Connell but Henry Howard, the Earl of Surrey, who was elected for the pocket borough of Horsham. Surrey's father, the Duke of

Right: The opulent and disorderly coronation banquet of George IV in July 1821 was the last to be held in Westminster Hall. Vast amounts of food and alcohol were consumed before the guests ransacked the building

less than six weeks after the bill was introduced in the Commons, and O'Connell celebrated 'The first day of freedom!' The Irish politician welcomed this 'bloodless revolution more extensive in its operation than any other political change that could take place.'

Although Wellington's government ushered in the Roman Catholic Relief Act for the sake of political expediency, they also

Norfolk, England's leading Catholic nobleman, also took his seat in the House of Lords. In July, O'Connell was re-elected for County Clare unopposed and entered the Commons under the new oath. He dedicated his energies at Westminster to repealing the Union, seeking the return of an independent Irish Parliament in Dublin.

⑥ Fire, Fire!

On the night of 16 October 1834 a massive fire ripped through the Palace of Westminster. As astonished crowds watched from the banks of the River Thames, the ancient buildings were razed to the ground

The fire began in the furnaces below the House of Lords. Two labourers had been hard at work all day, from seven o'clock in the morning, burning wooden 'tally sticks', an obsolete form of government accounting dating back to the Middle Ages. Thousands of these sticks were fed into the stoves hour upon hour. Parliament was not in session but when two visitors were shown into the Lords Chamber that afternoon they were alarmed that they could feel heat through their boots and that smoke was beginning to rise. The housekeeper assured them there was nothing to worry about since the floor was made of stone, but when she rebuked the labourers working below they said they were only obeying orders. At about five o'clock, after a hard day's work, the men went to slake their thirst with beer. An hour later someone raised the cry: 'Oh good God, the House of Lords is on fire.' Before the fire brigade arrived the Lords Chamber was gutted and the conflagration had spread to the rest of the parliamentary complex.

An eyewitness at Westminster reported in the *Times* newspaper:

'The spectacle was one of surpassing though terrific splendour … through a vista of flaming walls you beheld the Abbey frowning in melancholy pride over its defaced and shattered neighbours.' Soon the palace was a wreck. The fire brigade were hindered in

Above: *J.H. Foley's marble statue of Sir Charles Barry, architect of the new Palace of Westminster, shown studying his plans*

Facing page: *The House of Commons, formerly St Stephen's Chapel, was completely gutted by the fire of 1834*

their efforts by the unusually low tide on the River Thames which made it difficult to collect water to douse the flames. By the following morning many of the medieval buildings had

Act in 1832. Others, however, saw the disaster as a moment of opportunity. They celebrated the fire as the great climax of the reform process, sweeping away the ramshackle buildings which symbolized the corruption of a previous age. The radical politician William Cobbett (MP for Oldham) welcomed the inferno as 'a great event'.

Above: A large crowd gathered to watch as the fire brigade sought in vain to control the flames

been destroyed beyond repair, including the House of Lords, the House of Commons (St Stephen's Chapel), the Painted Chamber with its famous biblical wall paintings, and the cloisters. Nevertheless, the cavernous space of Westminster Hall with its thick walls and hammerbeam roof escaped unscathed.

A moment of opportunity

Some viewed the destruction of the Houses of Parliament as a sign of divine displeasure with the United Kingdom, perhaps heavenly retribution for the passing of the Roman Catholic Relief Act in 1829 or the Reform

The decimation of the old complex, which had grown up piecemeal over the previous 800 years, meant it was now possible to build from scratch. It was widely acknowledged that Parliament needed new facilities fit for the business of government in the 19th century. Britain was by now one of the world's great superpowers and demanded a Parliament Building to match its international prestige and to illustrate its national ideals. Fresh thinking was called for.

Some MPs, notably the Scottish radical Joseph Hume, campaigned for the removal of Parliament away from Westminster. The old location was notoriously inconvenient. It was noisy, damp, unhealthy, inaccessible and overpopulated. Raw sewerage poured from London's cesspits into the River Thames spreading disease and pollution, in a later generation resulting in 'the Great Stink' of 1858 which almost overpowered the Commons. The historic site was far too small and inconspicuous, hardly a symbol of pride for the Parliament of a world empire.

In an age of innovation and grandiose schemes, when much of London was being redeveloped, several commentators recommended beginning anew at Leicester Square, Charing Cross or St James' Park. King William IV also offered Buckingham Palace as a permanent replacement for Westminster Palace, but it was more suited to balls and banquets than parliamentary debate.

Eventually Parliament agreed to rebuild on the old site, despite its obvious limitations, in order to maintain its geographic and historic ties with Westminster Hall and Westminster Abbey. These two iconic structures were a visual reminder of the British Parliament's inextricable connections with the monarchy and the Christian church. It was precisely these links which some radicals hoped to sever by moving away from Westminster, but they lost the debate. It was also agreed that the new Parliament building should be neo-gothic, the architectural style which was at the height of fashion in the 1830s and in keeping with the abbey next door. Some wanted a neoclassic structure, reminiscent of the Roman senate, but this style was rejected because it was more associated with paganism than Christianity.

Inspiration and insanity

In June 1835 British architects were invited to submit designs for the new Houses of Parliament in an open competition. There were ninety-seven entries, many from budding young architects. The prize went to Charles Barry, aged 41, who had already established an international reputation with his churches, country mansions, and grand commissions such as the Travellers' Club in Pall Mall and Birmingham Grammar School. He chose to integrate surviving structures like Westminster Hall and the Chapel of St Mary's Undercroft within his plan for the parliamentary

Above: *The Palace of Westminster ablaze in October 1834*

The portcullis

Above: *The portcullis symbol is found throughout the Houses of Parliament*

The portcullis (a symbol of strength) was originally the badge of the Beaufort family, associated in the late 15th century with Lady Margaret Beaufort and her son, Henry VII. Tudor additions to the Palace of Westminster therefore often used the portcullis design along with roses, fleurs-de-lys and pomegranates. It is also a repeated motif within Henry VII's gothic chapel in Westminster Abbey.

The competition entries to rebuild the Houses of Parliament in the 1830s had to be pseudonymous, so Barry chose the portcullis as his logo.

He and Pugin saturated the new palace with this image, incorporating it thousands of times in their artistic details, and it thus became accepted during the 19th century as the symbol for Parliament. From 1967 the crowned portcullis has been used exclusively on Commons stationery, and in 1996 Queen Elizabeth II formally granted both Houses the right to use it as their badge. The emblem gives the name to Portcullis House, opposite the Palace of Westminster, which provides committee rooms and offices for MPs and was opened in 2001.

complex, which included not just new debating chambers but committee rooms, libraries, waiting rooms, dining rooms, offices and reception rooms.

At a time when political power in Britain was shifting away from the monarchy and the aristocracy towards the Commons, Barry's design drove in the opposite direction, harkening back to the *ancien régime*. He emphasised that the Houses of Parliament were first and foremost a royal palace, with the House of Lords as the architectural climax, and its central throne ready for the one day in the year when the monarch was present for the Opening of Parliament. He also decided to retain the old ecclesiastical shape of the House of Commons, which had become synonymous with

Westminster democracy. Barry estimated that the new buildings would be finished within six years, but in fact the work was drawn out over three decades.

As his principal draughtsman, Barry recruited A.W.N. Pugin, a precocious young architect with a love for medieval gothic. Pugin made his name as creator of prominent Roman Catholic buildings such as Birmingham Cathedral and St Patrick's College, Maynooth in Ireland. He was responsible for the internal decorations which embellished Barry's edifice, sketching out vivid designs ranging from the monarch's throne in the House of Lords and the Speaker's chair in the House of Commons, to minor details such as umbrella stands, gas lamps, inkwells and

Above: *The House of Lords, the architectural climax of Barry's scheme*

wallpaper. Yet his mental health collapsed under the pressure–his doctor claimed he had done a hundred years' work though he was not yet forty. In February 1852, the very month that Barry was knighted by Queen Victoria for his services to the nation, Pugin was certified insane and confined at Bethlehem Lunatic Asylum ('Bedlam'). By the autumn he was dead, leaving behind a young widow and eight children. Later Barry and Pugin's sons quarrelled in print about which man really deserved the plaudits as Parliament's architect.

Big Ben

The skyline of Barry's Houses of Parliament is dominated by three towers, in delicate architectural balance: the Victoria Tower, the Central Tower and the Clock Tower. The Victoria Tower was designed as the royal entrance to the palace and the repository for the parliamentary archives. At the time of its completion it was the largest and tallest square tower in the world, standing 325 feet (98.5 metres) high.

Above: *The Victoria Tower*

Below: Under each of the four clock faces a Latin prayer is carved in stone, 'Domine Salvam fac Reginam nostram Victoriam primam' ('O Lord, save our Queen Victoria the First')

Marginally shorter, at the opposite end of the palace, is the Clock Tower. There had once been a clock tower in the medieval palace and Barry renewed the tradition, probably modelled upon a prototype that Pugin designed for Scarisbrick Hall in Lancashire in 1837. It contains four quarter bells which chime on the quarter hours and one great bell ('Big Ben') which chimes every hour. The familiar melody of the quarter bells is known as the Westminster Chimes or the Westminster Quarters, though the simple tune was originally composed in the 1790s for the new clock at St Mary the Great Church in Cambridge. The four notes are matched by a traditional prayer: 'Lord through this hour / Be thou my guide / That by thy power / No foot shall slide.'

The great bell was probably named after Sir Benjamin Hall (First Commissioner for Works in the 1850s) whose name is inscribed on it. Though another possibility is Benjamin Caunt, a popular mid-Victorian boxer and pub landlord. The bell was cast at Norton near Stockton-on-Tees in August 1856 and transported by schooner from West Hartlepool to London, where it was welcomed by jubilant crowds. It was hung temporarily at the foot of the Clock Tower to be tested daily for a year, but in October 1857 the bell cracked. The foundry denied all responsibility and claimed the hammer was too heavy, so Big Ben was recast at Whitechapel before finally being raised into place. After chiming for a year another crack appeared and it fell silent until 1863 when the bell was rotated by ninety degrees so the hammer now strikes a different spot. The four foot (1.2 metre) crack in Big Ben can still be seen. Its iconic chimes were first broadcast by the BBC in 1923 and are regularly heard today on radio and television news bulletins.

The Fine Arts Commission

In 1841 Parliament established the Fine Arts Commission with responsibility for the decoration of the new Palace of Westminster. It was to be a building which celebrated British ideals portrayed by British artistic talent, both a national monument and at the same time a working Parliament. Barry wanted it to be 'a sculptured memorial of our national history'.

The commission was chaired by Queen Victoria's young consort, Prince Albert, whom she had wed at St James' Palace in February 1840. He was just twenty-two years old, but already an enthusiastic patron of the arts. However, the commissioners were criticized because many were politicians and none was a professional artist, except the secretary Sir Charles Eastlake (future president of the Royal Academy and director of the National Gallery). Some were also concerned that Albert's bias would mean his German compatriots received commissions for paintings or sculptures at Westminster. Foreign artists were therefore initially banned from contributing, though from 1844 the rules were eased to allow their participation if they had been resident in Britain for at least a decade.

The art work in Parliament was intentionally didactic. It was chosen to portray the greatness of Britain's heritage, both the development of its parliamentary democracy and its economic and military might. It sought to encapsulate the great founding narratives of British national identity, from Saxon times to the Battle of Waterloo. Many of the images were bound up with the romantic interpretation of the past beloved by the mid-Victorian generation, especially the revival of medieval Christian ideals as exemplified by the novels of Sir Walter Scott.

The House of Lords was the first to be decorated. Here six large frescos symbolize virtues associated with the three constituencies of the House: Chivalry, Religion and Justice, pointing to the interlocking relationship of the Lords Temporal, the Lords Spiritual and the Law Lords. For example, Religion is represented by the central image above the monarch's throne, painted by William Dyce. It shows the baptism in AD 597 by St Augustine of Canterbury of King Æthelberht of Kent, the first Saxon monarch to accept Christianity.

Above: *William Dyce's mural above the monarch's throne in the House of Lords, depicting the baptism of King Æthelberht of Kent, Britain's first Christian ruler*

Above: '*The Spirit of Religion' in the Lords Chamber, showing a king kneeling in prayer before the cross of Christ, as an archbishop reads from the Bible*

Below: *The Vision of Sir Galahad, from the Arthurian legend, one of William Dyce's murals in the Royal Robing Room*

Dyce was a favourite of Prince Albert and he was also commissioned to produce the frescos for the Royal Robing Room, the private chamber where the sovereign robes before the Opening of Parliament. The Prince wanted to demonstrate the connection between chivalry and monarchy so demanded images from the life of King Arthur, the legendary Christian king and British national hero. Dyce sought to represent seven aspects of chivalry: Religion, Generosity, Courtesy, Mercy, Hospitality, Courage and Fidelity (although only the first five were ever completed, due to the painter's death in 1864). Each virtue is illustrated with a historical narrative from the Arthurian romance. Again, the centrepiece facing the royal throne is Religion. It shows Sir Galahad, Sir Percival and Sir Bors, knights of the Round Table, who received a vision of Jesus Christ and the Four Evangelists at the start of their quest for the Holy Grail. This Arthurian iconography was developed further by eighteen bas-relief oak panels, carved by Henry Hugh Armstead.

'Unless the Lord builds the house'

The Fine Arts Commission aimed to establish a coherent and integrated scheme for the whole of the Palace of Westminster, throughout the halls, corridors, lobbies and committee rooms. The Prince's Chamber is dominated by portraits of the Tudor dynasty and bas-reliefs showing key historic events from the 16th century. The Peers Corridor and the Commons Corridor (leading from Central Lobby towards the Lords and Commons Chambers) are filled with paintings of the struggle for power between Parliament and the monarchy from the Civil War to the Glorious Revolution. Statues of royalty, soldiers, statesmen, scientists and poets also populate the palace.

Within the Royal Gallery, leading from the Royal Robing Room to the Lords Chamber, the dominant themes are regal and militaristic. It was perhaps intended as a British response to the Gallery of Battles, built at Versailles Palace in the 1830s to emphasize the glories of France. There were to be eighteen large murals with scenes from the triumphs of Queen Boudicca against the Romans, King Alfred against the Danes, Richard Coeur de Lion against Saladin, Queen Elizabeth against the Armada, the Duke of Marlborough against the French at Blenheim, and others. All these paintings were commissioned from Daniel Maclise, but by 1865 he had only completed the last two in the series, commemorating great British victories at Trafalgar and Waterloo during the Napoleonic Wars. The rest of his contract was cancelled.

Similar frustrations were experienced by John Rogers Herbert, who was commissioned to paint nine large frescos for the Peers Robing Room, to illustrate the foundations of the British legal system with scenes from Bible history. It was to include depictions of God's judgment upon Adam and Eve for their rebellion in the Garden of Eden, the giving of the Ten Commandments to Moses on Mount Sinai, the wisdom of Solomon, and the divine protection of Daniel in the den of lions. However, after fourteen

Below: St Stephen's Hall, with statues of prominent parliamentary statesmen

Above: Marble sculpture in the Prince's Chamber of Queen Victoria in her mid-30s, flanked by Justice and Clemency

Below: The Royal Gallery, dominated by Daniel Maclise's vast paintings of British victories in the Napoleonic Wars

years Herbert had only managed to complete the Moses mural and the rest of his commission was cancelled. So the room is known today as the 'Moses Room', used

by committees from the House of Lords. Towards the end of his life Herbert also finished 'The Judgement of Daniel', part of the original scheme which he gifted to Parliament in 1880. It portrays the apocryphal Old Testament story of Susanna, a virtuous Jewish woman rescued from the death penalty when Daniel proved the accusations against her were false.

Central Lobby, as the name suggests, is the centre point of the whole building. Here the commissioners chose to use Christian iconography to personify national ideals. Large mosaics portray the patron saints of the four constituent parts of the United Kingdom in the 19th century: St George for England, St David for Wales, St Andrew for Scotland and St Patrick for Ireland. Within the tiled floor is a verse from the Book of Psalms: '*Nisi Dominus aedificaverit domum, in vanum laboraverunt, qui aedificant eam*' (Psalm 127:1), a reminder to all who cross the threshold of the Houses of Parliament that 'unless the Lord builds the House, its builders labour in vain'. Other

Above: J.R. Herbert's painting of Moses on Mount Sinai, which gives the 'Moses Room' its name

Below: Herbert's 'Judgement of Daniel' which now hangs in the 'Moses Room'

quotations from the Bible were liberally emblazoned throughout the building. In the floor tiles of the Royal Gallery are the words: '*Cor Reginae in Manu Domini*' ('The heart of the Queen is in the hand of the Lord', Proverbs 21:1). The floor of the Commons Lobby bore the apostolic injunction: 'Fear God, Honour the Queen' (1 Peter 2:17), alongside Solomonic wisdom especially applicable to a parliamentary democracy, 'Without Counsel the People Fall; In the Multitude of Counsellors is Safety' (Proverbs 11:14).

New designs for a new generation

By the end of the 1850s the Fine Arts Commission was running out of steam. Their bold plans for hundreds of statues and paintings throughout the Houses of Parliament proved overambitious. The work was inevitably slower and more expensive than anticipated. Many of the commissioned artists lost enthusiasm for the project and the Chancellor of the Exchequer cut

off the funds. With the death of Barry in 1860 and Prince Albert in 1861, the commissioners limped on until Eastlake's death in 1865 but then collapsed. Some contracts were cancelled and other artists simply failed to produce what they had promised.

Above: *Central Lobby is dominated by mosaics of the four patron saints of the United Kingdom. Shown here is St Andrew of Scotland, designed in 1924*

Some of the commission's original designs were soon forgotten. For example, in St Stephen's Hall they wanted to depict 'the greatest epochs in our constitutional, social, and ecclesiastical history' from the 6th to the 16th century. There were to be ten murals, including the signing of *Magna Carta*, the abolition of serfdom, the conversion of the Anglo-Saxons to Christianity, and the English Reformation. In the

East Corridor paintings would illustrate ways in which the Christian gospel had liberated pagan Britain from 'ignorance, heathen superstition, and slavery' and how Christian values were exported to the British Empire in the 18th and 19th centuries. The commissioners wanted to emphasize that Britain had a God-given responsibility to bring Christian civilization to the rest of the world, with paintings depicting the arrival of Captain James Cook in Tahiti in 1769, the banning of the practice of suttee (a widow burned alive on her husband's funeral pyre) in India, and the emancipation of African slaves. These Victorian schemes were put on hold after Prince Albert's death, and never fulfilled. Before long such interpretations of Britain's history and national purpose had fallen out of favour.

In the 20th century the decoration of the Houses of Parliament was renewed. In 1910 the blank walls of the East Corridor were at last filled with scenes from Tudor England, and in 1924 a new Fine Arts Commission was set up to finish the work of its Victorian predecessor. Robert Anning Bell designed the final two patron saints (Scotland and Ireland) for Central Lobby, half a century after the first two (England and Wales) were designed by Edward Poynter. St Stephen's Hall was also decorated with a series of murals depicting 'The Building of Britain', which aimed 'to awaken us to the greatness and wonder of our growth as a nation, our evolution from a group of tribal states to a world-wide Commonwealth.' It was a deliberate attempt to help to restore national pride and confidence in British achievements after the devastation of the First World War and the social upheaval it caused.

A further series of sixteen large murals was commissioned from the renowned Anglo-Welsh painter, Frank Brangwyn, to complete the Royal Gallery. Rather than the scheme of militaristic conquest conceived in the 1840s, which no longer seemed so glorious after the horrors of the trenches, it would now depict the diverse productivity of the British Empire in a blaze of colour. Yet when the commissioners viewed the first five panels they rejected the work as out of keeping with the rest of the Houses of Parliament. The complete series was acquired in 1934 by the corporation of Swansea, where it now hangs in the Guildhall.

Another of the original hopes of the first Fine Arts Commission was to recreate the famous tapestries celebrating the English victory against the Spanish Armada. They were sold by Admiral Lord Howard of Effingham to King James I in 1616 and hung in the Lords Chamber until destroyed in the fire of 1834. The commissioners asked Richard Burchett to produce smaller recreations in paint for the Prince's Chamber, but he only completed one before his contract was cancelled. It took 150 years for the idea to be revived, financed by a private benefactor. Five more paintings based on engravings of the original Armada tapestries were recreated by Anthony Oakshett and installed in 2010.

Below: *Lollards (evangelical followers of the Bible translator John Wycliffe) gather secretly in the woods to read the Bible in English. Part of the 'Building of Britain' series of murals in St Stephen's Hall*

❼ Reform and representation

The process of parliamentary reform is never finished.
Political radicals in the 19th century continued to believe
that a better form of democracy was possible

Since the 1770s British radicals had begun to echo the impatient cry of the American colonists of 'no taxation without representation'. Thomas Paine's best-selling *Rights of Man*, banned until the 1820s, went so far as to advocate universal male suffrage on the philosophical premise that freedom to choose the government is one of humanity's natural rights. Although the revolutions in America and France provoked a conservative reaction at Westminster, the demand for electoral reform soon gathered pace, sometimes spilling over into violence. When the Prince Regent arrived to open Parliament in January 1817 he was faced by hostile crowds and two windows in his state coach were shattered, either by a stone or a bullet. In August 1819 there was disaster at a mass rally at St Peter's Fields in Manchester when the cavalry tried to arrest the speaker Henry Hunt, and eleven people were killed in the ensuing panic, nicknamed the 'Peterloo Massacre' in mock reference to the Battle of Waterloo. Parliament responded by passing the Six Acts, gagging radical newspapers and banning political meetings. These draconian measures provoked the Cato Street Conspiracy to murder the Prime Minister and his cabinet, but the plotters were discovered and either hung or transported.

The Great Reform Acts

When Earl Grey came to power at the head of a new Whig administration in November 1830, electoral reform was high on the agenda. Organisations like the London Radical Reform Association, the Metropolitan Political Union, and the National Union of the Working Classes demanded extension of the

Above: 'The Champions of Reform Destroying the Monster of Corruption', a satirical cartoon by James Gillray, published in 1831. The seven-headed dragon is an image for Satan in the Book of Revelation

Facing page: Earl Grey, author of the Great Reform Act of 1832

franchise and an end to historic inequalities. In the south of England many constituencies were 'rotten' or 'decayed' boroughs, small towns with a tiny electorate of less than fifty voters. Others were 'pocket' boroughs, in the 'pocket' of the aristocratic patron who nominated the local MP and no election took place. More than two hundred members of the Commons were baronets or sons of peers. At the same time, significant regions of the United Kingdom had little stake in the Westminster Parliament. Scotland had 45 MPs, only one more than Cornwall though it had six times the population. Major industrial cities like Manchester, Birmingham, Leeds and Sheffield had no parliamentary representation at all.

The government introduced a modest reform bill to reorganize the constituencies and to extend the franchise by a fraction. They argued that it was a necessary expedient to avoid revolution. Thomas Babington Macaulay warned that to reject the bill would result in 'the wreck of law, the confusion of ranks, the spoliation of property, and the dissolution of social order', but still the House of Lords threw it out. Angered by the intransigence of the unelected aristocracy, riotous mobs went on the rampage. At Nottingham the castle of the Duke of Newcastle was burned down; at Derby the gaol was razed to the ground; at Bristol the bishop's palace was destroyed. Still the Lords remained unmoved. Grey's son-in-law, Baron Durham, asked them: 'Are you prepared to live in solitude in the midst of multitudes, your mansions fortified with cannon … and protected by troops of faithful, perhaps, but, if the hour of danger come, useless retainers?' Only when the king promised to create enough new peers to force the bill

Above: *The House of Commons in 1832 at the time of the Great Reform Act, painted by Henry Melville*

Right: Queen Victoria at the Opening of Parliament in February 1845

Below: The bust of Richard Cobden, radical reformer and peace campaigner

through, did the Lords finally capitulate. So the Great Reform Act received royal assent in June 1832 and the electorate rose to approximately 800,000 (from 4,500 voters to 64,500 in Scotland). It was intended as the final solution to franchise reform, but was only the start of a long process which has continued to the present day.

Outside Parliament, agitation continued. In May 1838 the London Working Men's Association published their People's Charter, giving rise to the so-called 'Chartist' movement. They campaigned for six objects of reform including universal suffrage for men, secret ballots, and equal electoral districts. They wanted salaries for MPs and abolition of the property qualification for MPs, to enable working men to stand for Parliament. The Chartists also demanded a general election every year, to keep MPs accountable to the people so they could not 'defy and betray their constituents as now'. These ideas were neither new nor revolutionary, and they did not press for more radical ideas like votes for women or abolition of the House of Lords. Yet three times Parliament refused to consider their petitions.

In 1848, the 'year of revolutions' in continental Europe, a mass Chartist rally gathered at Kennington Common to march upon Westminster, but it was dispersed without trouble. This anticlimax signalled the collapse of the movement, having failed to influence parliamentary opinion. Macaulay, for example, warned that universal suffrage was 'fatal to all purposes for which government exists' and 'utterly incompatible with the very existence of civilisation'.

Above: *The bronze statue in Parliament Square of the Earl of Derby, who served as Prime Minister three times between 1852 and 1868*

Below: *Detail from a bronze bas-relief in Parliament Square depicting a cabinet meeting led by the Earl of Derby in 1867, at the time of the Second Reform Act*

By the mid-1850s the radical politician Richard Cobden was writing in despair: 'As for parliamentary reform, I hold that we might as well call out for the millennium' (that is, the return of Christ and the end of human history).

After the Chartist debacle, the reforming agenda was picked up again in the 1860s by the Reform Union and the Reform League. The League had over four hundred branches and 60,000 members, and held giant protest meetings in Hyde Park which sometimes descended into rioting. It gave birth to the Labour Representation League which campaigned to get working men elected to Parliament. Faced by these pressures, the Tory administration led by the Earl of Derby and Benjamin Disraeli grabbed the initiative in 1867 by driving through the Second Reform Act. It doubled the electorate and added many new voters to large urban constituencies.

Disraeli's parliamentary rival, William Gladstone, followed suit by introducing the secret ballot in 1872. Before this significant reform, all votes were cast in public which allowed landlords and employers to bully their tenants or workers to support a particular candidate. King William IV had once rejected the secret ballot as 'inconsistent with the manly spirit and the free avowal of opinion which

distinguish the people of England.' Others maintained that it would reduce the elector's responsibility to cast his vote wisely. Yet John Bright (Quaker MP and the first Nonconformist to serve in the cabinet) argued that secret voting would 'lessen expenses at elections, and greatly diminish corruption, and destroy the odious system of intimidation which now so extensively prevails.' Corruption and bribery were still rife, but were largely stamped out by the Corrupt and Illegal Practices Act which set strict limits on the amount of money candidates could spend during general elections.

Gladstone also ushered in the 1884 Franchise Act and 1885 Redistribution Act, known together as the Third Reform Act, a compromise between the Liberal and Conservative parties. It doubled the electorate to over five million, made voting qualification identical in boroughs and counties for the first time, gave most constituencies only one seat in the Commons instead of two, and began to equalize the size of electoral districts. The ratio of the largest to the smallest constituency shrank from 150:1 to 8:1. Now approximately two-thirds of all adult men in the United Kingdom were enfranchised. Joseph Chamberlain (President of the Board of Trade) celebrated these reforms as nothing less than 'a revolution … The centre of power has been shifted, and the old order is giving place to the new.'

Above: The marble statue of Benjamin Disraeli in the Members Lobby. At his feet is a pile of books, representing his contribution to literature as well as politics

Jewish emancipation

The Victorian reform movement encompassed not just changes to the electorate but also to the types of people allowed to take their seats in Parliament. At the start of the 19th century all MPs were required to take three separate oaths, designed as protection against specific political threats. The Oath of Supremacy (1534), dating from England's break with Rome at the Reformation, acknowledged the monarch's authority over the church. The Oath of Allegiance (1609), dating from the Gunpowder Plot, renounced the authority of the pope. The Oath of Abjuration (1701), after the Glorious Revolution, rejected the Jacobite claim to the throne and defended the Protestant succession. MPs were also required to denounce the Roman Catholic doctrines of transubstantiation, the invocation of the Virgin Mary and the saints, and the sacrifice of the mass, though this declaration was abolished by the 1829 Roman Catholic Relief Act. A new oath was devised for Catholic MPs, but the three traditional oaths remained in force for Protestants. From 1833 Quakers and Moravians were allowed to make a solemn affirmation rather than swear an oath, omitting the words 'So help me God', which enabled the industrialist, Joseph Pease, to become the first Quaker MP.

Nevertheless, by the middle of the century it was still true that only Christians, whether Protestant or Catholic, could serve in Parliament. People of other religions were excluded by the requirement to swear their loyalty to the crown 'on the true faith of a Christian' while holding a copy of the New Testament. A number of prominent Jews served in public office, but only after their conversion to Christianity. For example, Manasseh Lopes (a wealthy landowner in Devon) was baptized in the Church of England in 1802 and elected the same year as MP for the pocket borough of New Romney in Kent. Likewise Benjamin Disraeli was baptized in 1817, at the age of twelve, when his family converted to Christianity and therefore Parliament's religious tests were unproblematic when he was elected MP for Maidstone twenty years later.

Matters came to a head when Baron Lionel de Rothschild, from the Jewish banking dynasty, was elected as Liberal MP for the City of London in June 1847. The House of Commons granted him permission to take the oaths holding the Hebrew Tanakh (Old Testament) rather than the New Testament, but would not allow any variation in the form of words. Therefore Rothschild was excluded from his seat, though he continued to win the votes of his constituents in the elections of 1849, 1852, 1854 and 1857. Lord John Russell, Liberal Prime Minister and a longtime opponent of religious tests, introduced a Jewish Relief Bill in the Commons but it was blocked by the Lords. He was supported, amongst

Above: *The statue in Parliament Square of Benjamin Disraeli, a favourite of Queen Victoria. He was elevated to the House of Lords as the first Earl of Beaconsfield in 1876*

others, by Joshua Westhead (a leading Wesleyan MP) who argued that oaths were a useless way of maintaining Britain as a Christian nation. Westhead told the Commons that as a simple matter of justice Jews should be welcomed into Parliament, and quoted the words of Jesus Christ from the Sermon on the Mount: 'As ye would that men should do unto you, do ye even so unto them' (Matthew 7:12).

David Salomons, another leading member of Anglo-Jewry and Rothschild's cousin, adopted a different strategy in the campaign for emancipation. He was one of the first Jewish magistrates from 1838 and an alderman of the City of London from 1845. In June 1851 he was elected as MP for Greenwich but instead of refusing the parliamentary oaths he simply omitted the words 'on the true faith of a Christian' and took his seat until the Speaker forced him to withdraw. Salomons was excluded from the Commons and heavily fined, but soon he became the first Jewish Lord Mayor of London. The government finally agreed a compromise solution in the Oaths Bill of 1858, allowing each House to

Above: *Sir Joseph Boehm's marble statue of Lord John Russell, Liberal Prime Minister who campaigned for Jewish emancipation*

Below: *The House of Commons in session in 1858, with Viscount Palmerston at the dispatch box*

decide for itself what oaths to require of Jewish members. At last Rothschild was able to take his seat, and Salomons returned to the Commons in the general election the next year.

After 1858 the three historic oaths were combined into a single oath, further simplified in the 1860s. Almost all its religious content was purged away until it read as follows: 'I, A.B., swear by Almighty God that I will be faithful and bear true allegiance to Her Majesty Queen Victoria, her heirs and successors, according to law. So help me God.' This is still the form of oath required of MPs today (with the sovereign's name changed). The only people now excluded from Parliament by the oath are members of Sinn Féin who choose not to swear allegiance to the British crown.

Since Jewish emancipation, MPs have been permitted to take the parliamentary oath on a 'holy book' of their choice, which need not be the New Testament. When Dadabhai Naoroji, an Indian businessman, became Britain's first Asian MP in 1892, he swore the oath on his personal copy of the *Khordeh Avesta* (a sacred text

---

Liberating religion

Above: Caricature from 1871 of Edward Miall, campaigner for Nonconformist liberty

During the 19th century, Protestant Nonconformists used their growing influence in Parliament to tackle a series of historic grievances concerning the denial of religious liberty. Until 1836, Nonconformists were banned from registering births and deaths, or from conducting weddings in their own chapels. They were forced to pay compulsory rates towards the upkeep of the local Anglican parish church until 1868, and were banned from using parish burial yards until 1880. They were also excluded from Oxford and Cambridge universities, unable to take degrees until the mid-1850s or to hold college fellowships until 1871.

The most influential Victorian Nonconformist pressure group was the Society for the Liberation of Religion from State Patronage and Control, known for short as the 'Liberation Society'. It was headed by Edward Miall (MP for Rochdale from 1852) and campaigned unsuccessfully for the disestablishment of the Church of England and confiscation of its endowments. The Liberation Society also opposed government funding of faith schools, because Nonconformists' taxes were being used to support Anglican education. Today the Church of England remains established as the 'national church'. Its bishops and cathedral deans are appointed by the crown, on advice from the Prime Minister, and its most important synodical decisions are scrutinized and ratified (or rejected) by Parliament.

of Zoroastrianism). A century later, when Mohammad Sarwar became Britain's first Muslim MP in 1997, he swore the oath of allegiance on the Qur'an.

Imprisoned in the Clock Tower

The general election of 1880, the last titanic battle between Gladstone and Disraeli, resulted in a Liberal landslide. Amongst those swept into power was a prominent atheist and republican, Charles Bradlaugh, founder of the National Secular Society. He had grown up in the Church of England and taught in Sunday School, but came to reject Christianity and indeed any form of theism. He was elected as MP for Northampton, campaigning on a programme of economic

Above: F.W Pomeroy's statue in Central Lobby of William Gladstone, Britain's oldest Prime Minister

and parliamentary reform, despite the scaremongering of his opponents who called him 'the greatest enemy of God and of his truth now living amongst men'. During his second administration, Gladstone faced major international crises over Egypt, Sudan, South Africa and Ireland, but at home the Bradlaugh Affair proved a constant headache. Once again it focussed attention upon the breadth of the British Parliament, and rival conceptions of democracy and national identity.

Before Bradlaugh took the oath of allegiance as a new MP, he made the mistake of publishing a letter in *The Times* arguing that as an atheist it would be 'an act of hypocrisy' on his part to hold a Bible and swear by Almighty God, yet he would submit to this 'idle and meaningless' ceremony in order to take his seat. Such a provocative statement brought fierce denunciations in the Commons. Lord Randolph Churchill (Tory MP for Woodstock) warned the Liberal majority not to turn Parliament into 'a place where the solemn forms and practices of the Christian religion might be safely derided, and the existence of God publicly and with scorn denied.' After a heated debate, Bradlaugh was sent away without taking the oath.

A month later Bradlaugh returned to the Commons, demanding to be sworn-in. He was allowed to address the crowded chamber from the bar (the brass pole drawn across the aisle to show that he was

Above: Charles Bradlaugh, a political cartoon from 1880

technically outside the House), but then the Speaker commanded him to leave. Still he stood his ground, protesting that the order was illegal, even when his fellow MPs agreed by 326 votes to 38 that he must withdraw. The Speaker instructed the elderly Serjeant-at-Arms to remove him, but Bradlaugh shouted out in the ensuing chaos: 'I admit the right of the House to imprison me; but I admit no right on the part of the House to exclude me, and I refuse to be excluded.' He was arrested and taken to Parliament's private gaol (a room in the Clock Tower), the last person ever to be imprisoned by the House of Commons. They were comfortable quarters, where he was able to entertain his family and friends to dinner that evening,

before being released the next day. Amongst the many messages of support was a telegram sent to his cell from Stewart Headlam, an Anglican clergyman and pioneer Christian socialist. It read: 'Accept my warmest sympathy; I wish you good luck in the name of Jesus Christ, the emancipator, whom so many of your opponents blaspheme.'

Almighty God or Bradlaugh?

The place of religion in Parliament remained a major political question throughout the early 1880s. Some observed that there had already been atheist or skeptic MPs, even in the days of elaborate Christian oaths, such as Viscount Bolingbroke, Edward Gibbon and John Stuart Mill. It was estimated that at least fifty members of the Commons shared Bradlaugh's opinions on God's existence, though they did not proclaim their secularism in public. Comparisons were drawn with the recent emancipation of religious minorities like Nonconformists, Roman Catholics and Jews.

Nevertheless, Bradlaugh's opponents in the Commons were quick to point out that atheism was not merely a private belief, but had social and political consequences. One Liberal MP argued that if the state cut loose from religion it would be 'left a prey to all the immoralities and godlessness which will be sure to prevail among a community represented by men who have no belief in God.' Another warned, 'Admit the atheist, and you will have, in course of time, atheistical

Right: A third of the way up the Clock Tower is a prison room, where Charles Bradlaugh spent the night in June 1880 for defying the House of Commons

legislation.' Critics were quick to see links with Bradlaugh's republicanism, observing that atheism had led directly to the revolutionary overthrow of the French monarchy.

Hundreds of petitions flooded into Parliament from all sides. One letter sent to every MP even suggested that the borough of Northampton should be disenfranchised! The National Secular Society held protest meetings in defence of their president, and set up a 'League for the Defence of Constitutional Rights' and a 'Fund to Fight the Bigots'. The furore was viewed with bewilderment on the other side of the Atlantic, where the *Chicago Tribune* wryly observed that Americans preferred to choose their politicians like their architects, on the basis of ability rather than theological opinion. A New York newspaper denounced the House of Commons as 'the most bigoted assembly that exists in any part of the civilized world'. Yet British MPs continued to plead that 'a Christian country should be governed by Christian men.'

After Bradlaugh lost his legal challenges in the High Court, he took direct action. In August 1881 he arrived at Westminster amidst

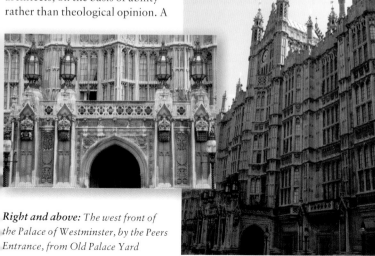

Right and above: The west front of the Palace of Westminster, by the Peers Entrance, from Old Palace Yard

Above: The Palace of Westminster looking north, viewed from the Victoria Tower

thousands of cheering supporters and tried to push his way into the Commons Chamber, shouting, 'I am here in accordance with the orders of my constituents, the electors of Northampton. Any person who lays hands on me will do so at his peril.' He was carried away by parliamentary officials and policemen, and dumped unceremoniously in the dust in Old Palace Yard with his clothes ripped. The crowd outside surged forward and it seemed momentarily as if they might storm the Houses of Parliament in defence of their champion.

Six months later Bradlaugh tried a startling new strategy. He walked calmly into the Commons carrying a New Testament and reciting the parliamentary oath, administering it to himself. He kissed the Bible, signed his name upon a sheet of paper which he left upon the Prime Minister's dispatch box, and declared, 'I tender that as the oath I have taken according to law'. The Commons was stunned. Amidst shouts of outrage, and cries of 'Order!' from the Speaker, the MP for Northampton sat down innocently on the Liberal benches. Gladstone called it 'the utmost scandal' and once again Bradlaugh was expelled, but he told the Commons: 'If I am not fit for my constituents they shall dismiss me, but you never shall. The grave alone shall make me yield.'

At the 1885 general election, the role of religious faith in public life became a key campaigning issue. One polemical pamphlet, entitled *Almighty God or Bradlaugh?*, warned that to allow the intrusion of atheism at Westminster would 'bring down the British constitution from the mountain top of Christianity, where it was placed by Alfred the Great, and where by the

Right: The Prime Minister's dispatch box in the House of Commons

Below: Queen Victoria in old age, at the Opening of Parliament in 1900

grace of God it has been kept ever since.' Yet in Northampton the constituents eagerly elected Bradlaugh yet again. When the new Parliament assembled in January 1886 to swear their oaths of allegiance to the crown, he joined the queue with his fellow MPs. This time there was a new Speaker in place, Sir Arthur Peel, youngest son of the former Prime Minister. Peel cut through the muddle by simply allowing

Bradlaugh to take the oath and by disallowing any objections. He kissed the Bible, inscribed his name on the roll, shook hands with the Speaker, and took his seat. The entire controversy was diffused at a stroke.

Bradlaugh pioneered the way for other atheists to follow. The 1888 Affirmation Act allowed anyone, not just Moravian and Quaker Christians, to make a non-religious affirmation of allegiance to the crown rather than swear an oath by Almighty God. For the first time this allowed non-religious men to take their place as MPs, justices of the peace, solicitors or barristers, without reference to God. In the House of Lords the first avowed atheist to make use of this provision was John Morley, Gladstone's biographer, who was elevated to the peerage in 1908.

⑧ Votes for all

Until the First World War the female half of the British population was banned from national political life, unable to vote or to stand for Parliament. Now it was their turn to agitate for reform

The movement for women's suffrage gathered momentum in the 1860s in the wake of the Second Reform Act. Manchester radicals like Lydia Becker, Jacob and Ursula Bright, Richard Pankhurst, and Elizabeth Wolstenholme helped to launch the Society for Women's Suffrage, which soon became a national campaign. In the House of Commons, John Stuart Mill attempted unsuccessfully to have the word 'person' substituted for 'man' in the 1867 reform bill. Shortly afterwards he published his last great political tract, *The Subjection of Women*, building on the principles already laid down in his classics, *On Liberty* (1859) and *Representative Government* (1861).

Nevertheless, the women's suffrage movement made limited progress in its early years. William Gladstone was personally opposed to giving women the vote and their enfranchisement played no part in his Third Reform Act. The 1888 Local Government Act, which created county councils, allowed women to vote and stand for office in local elections, but participation in parliamentary politics remained illusive. The National Union of Women's Suffrage Societies, led by Millicent Fawcett, worked patiently to build up support in the House of Commons and was winning the argument, but slowly.

Welfare Reform
In 1906 a new Liberal government came to power, led by Sir Henry Campbell-Bannerman, after a landslide in the general election. It marked an end to the dominance at Westminster of the Anglican gentry and a high point in the parliamentary influence of the Free Churches which were

Above: Prime Minister Campbell-Bannerman

Facing page: Memorial to Emmeline Pankhurst, militant campaigner for women's suffrage, unveiled outside the Houses of Parliament in March 1930 by Stanley Baldwin

Right: *Keir Hardie, Scottish lay preacher and one of the founders of the Labour Party*

support, especially from the trade unions. They were led by Keir Hardie, a former miner in the Scottish coal fields and an evangelical lay preacher. The Christian ethos he brought to the labour movement led Morgan Philips, a later general secretary of the Labour Party, to remark that 'Socialism in Britain owed more to Methodism than to Marx'.

Welfare reform was high on the government's agenda. On taking office Campbell-Bannerman vowed to make England 'less of a pleasure ground for the rich and more of a treasure house for the nation'. A raft of social legislation was enacted, laying the foundations of the modern Welfare State. They introduced free school meals for children, a minimum wage for miners, compensation for injury at work, and the right for trade unions to strike. Most significant were the 1908 Old Age Pensions Act which provided financial help for the elderly (promoted in Parliament by William Lever, Nonconformist MP and soap manufacturer) and the 1911 National Insurance Act which offered insurance against ill health or unemployment. MPs were also provided with salaries for the first time in 1911 (but not expenses) to enable working men to stand for Parliament, an old Chartist demand. Women's suffrage, however, was a bridge too far. Indeed many labour activists opposed the cause because it would merely multiply the number of wealthy voters in suburbia rather than enfranchise the working classes.

historically associated with civil and religious liberty and social justice. More than two hundred of the new MPs were members of Nonconformist denominations, about a third Congregationalists, more than at any time since the Commonwealth in the 1640s. At least 150 MPs were teetotal, a parliamentary record. One observer claimed that the House of Commons had become 'an organised army of Puritans'.

At the same time, commentators began to notice a decisive shift from religious consciousness to class consciousness as the dominant factor in British politics. The newly founded Labour Party won 29 seats at the 1906 election and began to capture the Liberal Party's traditional working class

Reforming the House of Lords

Old Age Pensions and other welfare reforms were funded by a radical taxation policy which explicitly aimed to redistribute wealth from the rich to the poor. The Chancellor of the Exchequer, David Lloyd George, defended his so-called 'People's Budget' of 1909 as a 'War Budget': 'It is for raising money to wage implacable warfare against poverty and squalidness.' He said it was time for 'robbing the hen roosts' by raising income tax and imposing death duties, which led one Tory opponent to accuse him of repealing the eighth and tenth Commandments against theft and covetousness!

The House of Lords threw out the proposals, provoking a constitutional crisis. It was the first time since the 17th century that the Lords had challenged the right of the Commons to control national finances. So the government called a snap election in which the power of the Lords was the key issue. They argued that an unelected hereditary chamber should not be able to oppose the people's elected representatives. The result of this controversy was the 1911 Parliament Act, which ensured that the Lords could not reject or amend any bill concerning money, nor block any other bill for more than two years (reduced to one year in 1949). These were radical restrictions on the historic powers of the Lords, but they capitulated when King George V threatened to create hundreds of new peers to force it through.

Above: *MPs relax on the terrace of the House of Commons, overlooking the Thames, painted by Emily Childers in 1909. Keir Hardie is second from the left, leaning on the parapet*

The Parliament Act also stated that the hereditary nature of the second chamber would soon be abolished. Lloyd George ridiculed the Lords as 'Five hundred men, chosen randomly from among the ranks of the unemployed.' Yet the promised reforms never took place. The creation of 'life peers' from 1958 shifted the balance more towards an appointed chamber, but not until the 1999 House of Lords Act were most hereditary peers expelled. Under a compromise agreement ninety-two hereditary peers were allowed to remain, on an interim basis, until Parliament agreed the future of the Upper House.

'Votes for Women'

The Women's Social and Political Union (WSPU) was one of many organizations campaigning for women's suffrage. It was founded by Richard Pankhurst's widow, Emmeline, supported by her three daughters, Christabel, Sylvia and Adela. The WSPU sought complete political equality between women and men, but when the government refused to listen they turned to militancy. Adopting the slogan 'Votes for Women', they conducted a campaign of social disobedience, disruption and escalating violence from October 1905. Emmeline Pankhurst told the Prime Minister that a growing number of women were willing 'to sacrifice even life itself' to win the vote. The *Daily Mail* coined the term 'suffragette' to distinguish these militants from the peaceful 'suffragists' who preferred to use constitutional methods to influence Parliament.

Suffragette tactics included mass demonstrations, heckling of politicians, setting pillar boxes on fire, attacking railway trains and smashing the windows of shops and public buildings. As Emmeline Pankhurst put it: 'The argument of the broken pane of glass is the most valuable argument in modern politics.' They chained themselves to the railings outside 10 Downing Street, disrupted debates in the House of Commons, and moored a steam launch on the Thames alongside Parliament's riverside terrace to harangue MPs while they drank their tea. The suffragettes were regularly involved in pitched battles with the police. On one occasion when confronted by mounted police

Above: Emmeline Pankurst is arrested at a suffragette demonstration outside Buckingham Palace in 1914

Below: The statue of Viscount Falkland in St Stephen's Hall still bears the damage, in the form of a broken spur from his boot, caused when a suffragette chained herself to it in April 1909

in Parliament Square, Emmeline proclaimed that they would not 'shrink from death … If the government brings out the Horse Guards and fires on us, we will not flinch.'

The WSPU aimed at maximum publicity and popular sympathy. They deliberately courted arrest, often assaulting policemen to make sure they were sent to gaol. Soon an entire wing of Holloway Prison in north London was filled with suffragettes. In October 1908 Emmeline and Christabel were arrested with Flora Drummond for urging a crowd at Trafalgar Square to 'rush the House of Commons'. Their trial became a *cause célèbre* during which Christabel told the court: 'We are here, not because we are law-breakers; we are here in our efforts to become law-makers.' The *Daily Mirror* observed that 'Parliament has never granted any important reform without being bullied.'

Above: *The prisoners' badge adopted by the Women's Social and Political Union, combining the parliamentary portcullis with the broad arrow (symbolizing prisoners of the crown)*

The most controversial suffragette tactic was the hunger strike. In July 1909 Marion Wallace-Dunlop was convicted and sent to Holloway for stamping an extract from the 1689 Bill of Rights on the wall of St Stephen's Hall using a printing block and indelible violet ink. In protest she refused the prison food and was released after 91 hours of fasting. When other suffragettes adopted the same strategy, the authorities responded with forcible feeding, a violent and invasive procedure which involved being held down by medical staff and fed through a tube. Emmeline Pankhurst joined the ranks of hunger strikers and later wrote in her autobiography: 'Holloway became a place of horror and torment. Sickening

scenes of violence took place almost every hour of the day, as the doctors went from cell to cell performing their hideous office.'

There was public outcry at this barbaric treatment. In the House of Commons one Labour MP, George Lansbury, denounced Prime Minister Asquith in June 1912: 'You will go down to history as the man who tortured innocent women. You ought to be driven from public life.' Lansbury was suspended from the Commons for this outburst, and soon lost his seat, though he later rose to be leader of the Labour Party. In March 1913 Parliament introduced the Prisoners (Temporary Discharge for Ill-Health) Act, nicknamed 'The Cat and Mouse Act', which enabled them to release hunger striking suffragettes and then rearrest them a week later to continue their sentences. As a result many women were in and out of Holloway Prison like yo-yos, which made the government look foolish and persecuting.

Right: *Marble statue of Herbert Henry Asquith, a doughty opponent of women's suffrage*

During 1913 the publicity stunts of the WSPU became increasingly dramatic. A package was posted to Lloyd George containing sulphuric acid and it burst into flames when it was opened. Three weeks later a new house he was building at Walton-on-the-Hill in Surrey was blown up by the suffragettes and Emmeline Pankhurst was sentenced to three years penal servitude when she claimed responsibility. She told the judge at her Old Bailey trial: 'I have no sense of guilt. I look on myself as a prisoner of war.' In June, Emily Davison launched a fatal protest at the Epsom Derby. She rushed on to the course and tried to grab the bridle of the king's horse, *Anmer*, but was knocked down, suffered a fractured skull and died four days later. Her gravestone bears the motto, 'Deeds not words'. The following spring Mary Richardson attacked Diego Velázquez's painting of the *Rokeby Venus* in the National Gallery, slashing it with a meat cleaver. The suffragettes also planted a bomb at Westminster Abbey which damaged the Coronation Chair. Meanwhile Sylvia Pankhurst threatened to starve herself to death outside the House of Commons. Christabel Pankhurst even suggested burning down Nottingham Castle, as a previous generation of political radicals had succeeded in doing before the Reform Act of 1832.

Christian militancy

The suffragettes often described their campaign in theological language, using Christian motifs. Some of their more peaceful methods, such as open air rallies, mass processions and the distribution of tracts, were adopted directly from Victorian revivalist movements like the Salvation Army. They portrayed their quest for women's emancipation as a holy war, denouncing opponents as Pharisees or even Antichrists. The female French revolutionary Jeanne d'Arc (beatified by the Pope in 1909), was prominent in suffragette pageants as the archetypal Christian militant. Her motto: 'Fight On, and God will Give the Victory', was embroidered on the banner carried by young girls at the front of Emily Davison's carefully choreographed funeral procession through Bloomsbury. Meanwhile those who suffered forcible feeding in Holloway Prison were likened to the martyrs of the early church.

Above: Sir Jacob Epstein's bronze of Ramsay MacDonald, first Labour Prime Minister in the 1920s, in the Members Lobby

Many suffragettes were eager to combine Christian principles with social reform. They saw the emancipation of women as a natural consequence of the revolutionary agenda of the New Testament, and even identified their methods with those of Christ. One member of the WSPU told the Archbishop of Canterbury: 'Let me remind you … Christ was a lawbreaker, a moral revolutionary and was crucified as a felon. There is no blame unctuously pronounced by the Church and State against us that could not have been pronounced against Him.' Likewise Davison prophesied in *The Price of Liberty*, one of her best known and posthumously published essays, that some suffragettes would be forced to choose death and thus 're-enact the tragedy of Calvary for generations yet unborn'. Christian denominations began their own campaign groups, like the Church League for Women's Suffrage with 5,700 members, including more than 500 Anglican clergymen. After parliamentary franchise was won, it was rebranded the League of the Church Militant and began to agitate for women's ordination, encouraged by leading suffragists like Millicent Fawcett and Emmeline Pethick-Lawrence.

Victory at last

When the Great War broke out in August 1914, Christabel Pankhurst declared in *The Suffragette* that the international conflict was 'God's vengeance upon the people who held women in subjection'. Nevertheless, as a sign of its patriotic fervour, the WSPU announced the suspension of its militant campaign and threw its energies behind the war effort. This was an abrupt but shrewd change of tactics, which helped to swing public opinion in their favour. The government had already begun to recognize that it was impossible to resist the enfranchisement of women for ever.

A new coalition government, led by Lloyd George, piloted the Representation of the People Bill

Right: Plaque commemorating Emily Davison's act of defiance when she hid in a cupboard near the Chapel of St Mary's Undercroft on the night of the national census in April 1911

Right: Nancy Astor, the first woman to sit in Parliament

through Parliament in January 1918, known as the Fourth Reform Act. For the first time it gave the vote to women over the age of thirty and also, just as significant, to all adult men regardless of property. Many of the soldiers who put their lives on the line in the trenches, for the sake of king and country, were not previously entitled to vote. Seventy years after the Chartist campaigns, manhood suffrage had arrived at last (although conscientious objectors who refused to fight in the war were disfranchised for five years). At a stroke, the size of the electorate more than doubled from 8 million to 21 million.

At the general election in December 1918, a month after Armistice Day, seventeen women stood as candidates for Parliament. The only one elected was Countess Constance Markievicz, an Irish republican who had been sentenced to death for her part in the 1916 Easter Rising (commuted to penal servitude because of her sex), but she refused to take her seat at Westminster. Christabel Pankhurst seemed certain to become Britain's first woman MP but she made the mistake of contesting the working class constituency of Smethwick in the West Midlands and was narrowly beaten by the Labour candidate, a local union official.

History was made a year later when Nancy Astor became the first woman MP after a by-election in Plymouth, stepping into her husband's seat when he became a viscount. Churchill saw it as an intrusion upon Parliament's all male preserve and later remarked, 'I felt like a woman had entered my bathroom and I had nothing to protect myself with except a sponge.' Ironically, Astor had paid little interest in the suffrage movement and was best known as a society hostess. She was joined in 1921 by Margaret Wintringham who also inherited her seat from her MP husband, after he suddenly collapsed and died at the House of Commons.

New priorities

After her defeat in the 1918 election, Christabel Pankhurst began a second career as a Christian author and preacher, after beginning serious study of the Bible and evangelical theology. She spoke to huge crowds on both sides of the

Right: Memorial in Victoria Tower Gardens to Christabel Pankhurst, suffragette and evangelical preacher

Atlantic and penned popular books like *The Lord Cometh: The World Crisis Explained* (1923), which went through seven editions in five years. Pankhurst saw this new ministry as entirely consistent with her previous campaigns for gender equality, but had come to the realization that votes for women was not a panacea to solve the ills of society. The huge death toll of the First World War convinced her that humanity's greatest need was not political reform but 'the cross of Christ for redemption of sin and His second coming to deliver the world from war and unrighteousness.'

In a speech in London in 1926 Christabel Pankhurst observed that 'however good were the intentions of the advocates of equal rights for women, they had overlooked the fact that what mankind needs is not a change of conditions but a change of heart.' Her mother, Emmeline, came to the same conclusion: 'We thought a miracle was going to happen; all reformers think that. We thought it was going to bring Utopia, but we left human nature out of the question.' Christabel saw the answer in the coming of the

Pioneering parliamentary women

When women under the age of thirty were finally enfranchised in 1928, the number of female MPs jumped from 4 to 14 at the next general election. However, half a century later, in 1979, there were still only 19 women in the House of Commons (one of whom was the Prime Minister). Not until the late 1980s did the number begin to rise sharply. Sixty women were returned to Parliament in the general election of 1992, which doubled to 120 in the Labour landslide five years later. After the 2010 election, there were 142 women MPs, a new record but still only 22% of the total membership of the Commons.

Amongst the women who have broken into new territory are the following parliamentary 'firsts':

1919 Member of the House of Commons (Nancy Astor)
1929 Cabinet Minister (Margaret Bondfield)
1958 Member of the House of Lords (Baroness Swanborough, Baroness Wootton)
1979 Prime Minister (Margaret Thatcher)
1981 Leader of the House of Lords (Baroness Young)
1992 Speaker (Betty Boothroyd)
1997 Northern Ireland Secretary (Mo Mowlam)
2006 Foreign Secretary (Margaret Beckett)
2006 Lord Speaker (Baroness Hayman)
2007 Home Secretary (Jacqui Smith)
2010 Speaker's Chaplain (Rose Hudson-Wilkin)

Kingdom of God: 'Whether it be a Lloyd George or a Macdonald, a government violently Red or ultra-conservative or moderate or liberal, or a government of women, and you know we may some time have a government of women even – any British government in these days will have a burden upon its shoulder which can only be borne by the Son of God.' In *The Lord Cometh* she reiterated that even a modern democratic Parliament was 'wholly unable ... even to form, much less to put into effect, a policy that will regenerate the world.'

Blitzkrieg

During the early phases of the Second World War, London was subjected to air raids night after night. The Houses of Parliament suffered bomb damage on fourteen separate occasions.

Windows were blown out and masonry demolished. One blast threw Richard Coeur de Lion from his pedestal, fracturing his sword. During 1940 and early 1941 Parliament convened in Church House, Westminster (the Church of England's assembly rooms, built in the 1930s) for fear that the Commons and Lords might be deliberately targeted while they were sitting and the nation's entire political leadership wiped out at one stroke.

Then on the night of 10–11 May 1941 the Palace of Westminster was set alight by incendiary bombs dropped by the Luftwaffe. One bomb hit the Clock Tower. Another struck the Lords Chamber but passed straight through the floor without exploding. Yet the Commons Chamber and the roof of Westminster Hall were ablaze. It was impossible to save both,

Above: The fire-damaged arch leading into the House of Commons, a permanent reminder of the blitzkrieg which destroyed the original building. It is flanked by statues of Churchill and Lloyd George

so the fire brigade focussed their rescue efforts on the medieval hall. By the next morning the Commons was a burnt out shell, a mound of rubble and timber. Little could be salvaged. Found amongst the embers was a charred Bible which was re-presented to the House in 1991 and is now kept within the opposition dispatch box. The Commons moved to the Lords Chamber, and the Lords to the Royal Robing Room, until new facilities could be built.

As with the fire of 1834, the bombing of the Commons in 1941 offered a rare opportunity to think afresh about the style and location of Britain's Parliament. Some wanted to adopt the semicircular arrangement favoured by most legislatures outside the British Commonwealth, like the United States Senate. Nancy Astor believed this would help to diffuse the confrontational nature of debate in the Commons, so that MPs 'did not have to sit and look at each other, almost like dogs on a leash, and that controversy would not be so violent.' James Maxton (leader of the Independent Labour Party) went further. He suggested that the ruins of the Commons be left as a historic monument at Westminster and that Parliament be rebuilt twenty miles outside London, with its own railway station, car park and airport, ready for the 'new world' which would be ushered in after the war.

Yet Churchill argued passionately that the Commons should be rebuilt in its old style, modelled on a Christian chapel, significant in the development of Britain's two-party democracy. He told his fellow MPs: 'We shape our buildings and afterwards our buildings shape us.' He also liked the tradition of an overcrowded room which was too small for all its members, to encourage 'a sense of intimacy'. So although the galleries were extended to create more room for visitors and the press, the floor of the House stayed exactly the same size, with only 427 seats for 646 MPs.

Sir Giles Gilbert Scott was commissioned to redesign the Commons in continuity with the

Above: Ivor Roberts-Jones' bronze statue of Sir Winston Churchill in Parliament Square

Independence and devolution

Throughout the 18th and 19th centuries, political power in the United Kingdom was increasingly centralized at Westminster. The Scottish Parliament at Edinburgh was dissolved by the 1707 Act of Union, as was the Irish Parliament at Dublin in 1801. Yet during the 20th century this process was reversed.

Irish nationalist MPs, like Daniel O'Connell and Charles Stewart Parnell, were particularly vocal in demanding the return of Dublin's independence. Outside Parliament Fenian terrorists resorted to violence, such as the murder of Lord Frederick Cavendish in Phoenix Park, Dublin in May 1882 on the day he was sworn in as Chief Secretary for Ireland. Three years later Fenian explosions rocked Westminster Hall and the Commons Chamber, though the House was not in session so injuries were few. Gladstone introduced 'Home Rule' bills in 1886 and 1893 to devolve responsibility for domestic Irish affairs to a new Dublin Assembly, but he was twice defeated.

Ireland at last won its independence from the United Kingdom in 1922. However, Northern Ireland opted instead for 'Home Rule', with devolved powers and a new bicameral Parliament at Stormont in Belfast. This arrangement continued for half a century until the Parliament was abolished in 1973 at the height of the 'Troubles' during which hundreds of Catholics and Protestants were killed. Meanwhile Westminster was targeted again by dissident Irish republicans. In June 1974 a bomb planted in Westminster Hall by the Provisional Irish Republican Army (IRA) injured eleven people and caused extensive damage. Then on 30 March 1979 the Irish National Liberation Army (INLA) planted a bomb under the car of Airey Neave (shadow Secretary of State for Northern Ireland), a close ally of Margaret Thatcher. It exploded as he drove out of the House of Commons car park and he died an hour later in Westminster Hospital. Neave is the only politician to be remembered by a memorial plaque in the Commons Chamber.

The Northern Ireland Assembly was revived following the 1998 Good Friday Agreement. At the same period legislative and fiscal powers were devolved from Westminster to the Scottish Parliament in Edinburgh and the Welsh Assembly in Cardiff, following referendums in those countries.

Left: Demolition of the blitzed House of Commons after the Second World War

style of Barry and Pugin, though neo-gothic architecture had long since fallen out of fashion. It therefore stands today in sharp contrast to modernist edifices like the Royal Festival Hall, raised on the South Bank to host the 1951 Festival of Britain. Both buildings, on opposite sides of the River Thames, symbolize in their own way British revival and recovery after the traumas of the Second World War.

Rising from the ashes

The rebuilt Commons was officially opened on 26 October 1950. At Churchill's suggestion the old fire-damaged arch leading into the Commons Chamber from the Commons Members Lobby was retained as 'a monument to the ordeal which Westminster has passed through', but the rest was new. The furniture was donated by former dominions and colonies within the Commonwealth, a sign of the esteem with which they viewed the British Parliament and the widespread influence of the 'Mother of Parliaments' on the democratic government of many nations. The Speaker's chair came from Australia, the clerks' table from Canada, the clerks' chairs from South Africa, the two dispatch boxes from New Zealand, the Serjeant-at-Arms' chair from Ceylon (Sri Lanka), the entrance doors from India and Pakistan, the furniture for the division lobbies from Nigeria and Uganda, the bar of the House from Jamaica, with ink stands, ashtrays, table lamps, chamber clocks and other furniture from elsewhere around the world.

Many Speakers from Commonwealth legislatures were present for the opening ceremony. As always, a service of prayer preceded the day's business, but after the traditional liturgy the Dean of Westminster added a special petition for the occasion. Seeking God's blessing on all the

Below: *The Parliament of New Zealand donated the new dispatch boxes at which the Prime Minister and Leader of the Opposition address the Commons*

proceedings in the new chamber, he prayed, 'We thank thee for the goodly heritage bequeathed to us by those who in times past have served thee in this place, and we pray that entering into their labour we may be found worthy guardians of the honour of this House. Guide and control, we beseech thee, our deliberations, making us so mindful of our trust that truth and righteousness, justice and liberty may ever flourish and abound, and the people of this realm may find their perfect freedom in thy service.'

Below: The Speaker's chair in the new House of Commons, donated by the Australian Parliament

The Dean's prayer was a bold affirmation of the spiritual, as well as political, responsibilities of the Westminster Parliament. Looking to the future, he reminded the gathered MPs and other dignitaries of the central role of the Christian faith in British public life and public discourse. That partnership has been illustrated for the last millennium by the close geographical connection between Westminster Palace and Westminster Abbey, symbolizing the enduring relationship between church and nation.

'Truth and righteousness, justice and liberty' have not always flourished in national life, and have sometimes been obscured by the actions of Parliament and the church, but they remain foundational Christian virtues. Countless parliamentarians down the generations have thus understood their public service as part of their service of God. Still today, those long centuries of Christian heritage are demonstrated for all to see by the art, architecture, traditions and ideals of the Houses of Parliament.

TRAVEL INFORMATION FOR PARLIAMENT SQUARE

See the map of Westminster inside the front cover and the floor plan of the Houses of Parliament inside the back cover

Houses of Parliament

www.parliament.uk
Guided tours through the Houses of Parliament usually visit the Royal Robing Room, Royal Gallery, Prince's Chamber, House of Lords and House of Commons (unless either House is sitting), Central Lobby, St Stephen's Hall and Westminster Hall. Overseas visitors may book tickets on Saturdays and during the summer months when Parliament is in recess. UK residents may also book a guided tour at other times of the year through their local MP or a peer. It is also possible to listen to parliamentary debates in the Commons and the Lords for free, from the public galleries, though space is limited.

Jewel Tower

www.english-heritage.org.uk
The Jewel Tower was built in the 1360s during the reign of Edward III on land appropriated from

Westminster Abbey to house the crown jewels and plate. The archives of the House of Lords were kept here in the early 19th century, which saved them from destruction in the fire of 1834.

Westminster Abbey

www.westminster-abbey.org
Westminster Abbey is a royal peculiar, under the direct jurisdiction of the British sovereign. It was re-founded in 1065 by Edward the Confessor and has been the place for every coronation since. For five hundred years between Henry III in 1272 and George II in 1760 most kings and queens were buried in the abbey. It is also the final resting place of many luminaries from British national life, including Geoffrey Chaucer, Isaac

Newton, David Garrick, William Pitt, William Wilberforce, Charles Barry, Charles Dickens, David Livingstone, Charles Darwin and William Gladstone.

St Margaret's Church, Westminster

www.westminster-abbey.org/st-margarets
In the shadow of Westminster Abbey stands St Margaret's Church, often known as 'the parish church of the House of Commons'. Between 1660 and 1832 the Commons adjourned here several times a year to listen to sermons marking the Gunpowder Plot, the martyrdom of Charles I, the restoration of Charles II and other royal anniversaries. When Armistice was announced on 11 November 1918, Lloyd George led

Left: *The Jewel Tower*

the Commons to St Margaret's for prayers of thanksgiving, a precedent followed by Winston Churchill at the end of the Second World War.

Westminster Central Hall

www.methodist-central-hall.org.uk

Westminster Central Hall, opposite Westminster Abbey, was opened in 1912 as the headquarters of the Wesleyan Methodist Church. It was designed as a grand monument to mark the centenary of the death of John Wesley in 1791, deliberately built in baroque style without overt religious symbolism so as not to resemble a church. The Hall has been the venue for many significant political rallies and was requisitioned for the inaugural General Assembly of the United Nations in 1946. Its basement was the largest air raid shelter in England during the Second World War.

Westminster Arms

The Westminster Arms is the local public house for Members of Parliament. Here the visitor is likely to rub shoulders with Honourable Members taking a break from duty.

Above: The Lady Chapel of Westminster Abbey, commissioned by Henry VII at the beginning of the 16th century

Left: The western entrance to Westminster Abbey. The gothic lower part was completed in the 15th century, but the towers were added by Nicholas Hawksmoor in the 1730s

Timeline

960s	Westminster Abbey founded
1066	Death of Edward the Confessor
1090s	Westminster Hall built
1215	Signing of *Magna Carta*
1290s	St Stephen's Chapel built
1376	First 'Speaker' of the Commons
1399	Richard II deposed
1529	Henry VIII departs from Westminster Palace
1535	Trial of Sir Thomas More
1559	Elizabethan Settlement
1605	Gunpowder Plot
1629	Charles I begins his 'Personal Rule'
1642	Civil War begins
1648	Pride's Purge
1649	Execution of Charles I
1653	Barebone's Parliament
1654	Oliver Cromwell elected as Lord Protector
1660	Monarchy and House of Lords restored
1678	Popish Plot
1689	Bill of Rights
1707	Scottish Parliament merged with Westminster
1780	Gordon Riots
1801	Irish Parliament merged with Westminster
1807	Slave Trade Abolition Act
1812	Assassination of Spencer Perceval
1833	Slavery Abolition Act
1828	Test and Corporation Acts repealed
1829	Roman Catholic Relief Act
1832	Great Reform Act
1834	Fire destroys the Houses of Parliament
1838	People's Charter
1858	Jewish emancipation
1867	Second Reform Act
1880	Charles Bradlaugh elected to Parliament
1882	Law courts move away from Westminster
1885	Third Reform Act
1905	Rise of the Suffragette Movement
1918	Fourth Reform Act
1941	Houses of Parliament blitzed
1950	House of Commons reopened

Above: The Houses of Parliament at dusk

FURTHER READING

The Bradlaugh Case. Walter Arnstein. (University of Missouri Press, 1983)

A History of Parliament: The Middle Ages. Ronald Butt (Constable, 1989)

Charles I. Charles Carlton. (Routledge, 1995)

The Story of Parliament in the Palace of Westminster. John Field. (Politicos, 2002)

The Gunpowder Plot. Antonia Fraser. (Weidenfeld & Nicolson, 1996)

Westminster Hall. Dorian Gerhold. (James & James, 1999)

Chaplain to Mr Speaker. Donald Gray. (HMSO, 1991)

William Wilberforce. William Hague. (HarperCollins, 2007)

The Assassination of the Prime Minister. David Hanrahan. (Sutton, 2008)

King Mob. Christopher Hibbert. (Sutton, 2004)

Catholic Emancipation. Wendy Hinde. (Blackwell, 1992)

Christabel Pankhurst. Timothy Larsen. (Boydell, 2002)

Parliament under the Tudors. Jennifer Loach. (Clarendon, 1991)

The Rise of Democracy in Britain, 1830-1918. Ian Machin. (Macmillan, 2001)

The Pankhursts. Martin Pugh. (Allen Lane, 2001)

The Houses of Parliament. Christine and Jacqueline Riding (eds). (Merrell, 2000)

The Stuart Parliaments 1603-1689. David Smith. (Arnold, 1999)

ACKNOWLEDGEMENTS

The author, editor and publisher would like to express particular appreciation for the cooperation of members of the Curator's Office (Palace of Westminster), Parliamentary Archives, and the support and help of David Landrum, Julian Dee, and Nick Battley.

Picture acknowledgements

All photographs of art and architecture inside the Houses of Parliament are copyright of the Palace of Westminster Collection and are published with permission. Thanks also to Deryc Sands for photographs on pages 17 and 42.

The facsimile on page 30 © Parliamentary Archives, London. HC/CL/JO/1/5
Pages 4–5 © Derek J Prime
Yeomen of the Guard on page 33 © Dan Kitwood/Getty Images.
Emmeline Pankhurst on page 113 © Jimmy Sime/Hulton Archive/Getty Images.

AUTHOR

Dr Andrew Atherstone is tutor in history and doctrine, and Latimer research fellow, at Wycliffe Hall, Oxford. He is a member of Oxford University's theology faculty and a fellow of the Royal Historical Society. He has published widely on aspects of British ecclesiastical history, especially in the 19th and 20th centuries, and has also contributed *The Martyrs of Mary Tudor* (second edition, 2007) and *Travel Through Oxford* (2008) in this Travel Guide series.

Left: Inside the Westminster Arms, the bell rings to give notice of a division in the House